NOTHING IS IMPOSSIBLE

Caspar McCloud

Endorsements

"Caspar McCloud is an amazing guitarist."

~ Mark Lee, Third Day

"I've never met anyone quite like Caspar McCloud. I hope his story blesses you as much as he has blessed me."

~ Peter Furler, The Newsboys

"Caspar has lived the life of a rock star and renowned painter. He has struggled with some of the most painful issues any of us can face. He has known life and death. At one point his heart literally stopped and God resuscitated him. His story is a gripping read because his struggles reflect God's grace and power."

~ Seth Barnes, Author and Founder
Adventures in Missions

"After one doctor stated he didn't believe Caspar could perform safely, he dared to trust God Almighty and perform anyway. Caspar fainted and at one point had no pulse. Pastor Henry Wright then prayed and his pulse returned." Another doctor said Caspar hasn't had an irregular heartbeat since! To learn how he

now performs and encourages people about God's healing power you must read this book!"

~ Michelle Morey, Associate Producer
TBN Television's "Night of Miracles"

"*Caspar McCloud floats in the clouds -- heavenly music, spiritual inspiration, a gentle spirit in touch with his God.*"

~ Robert Lacey, Best-Selling Author and Royal Biographer by Appointment to Queen Elizabeth II

"*Caspar McCloud is a great guitarist, singer and songwriter.*"

Matt Bassionett, Joe Satriani Band – G3-Ringo Starr – All Star Band

"*We all love a story! And when that story is true it only enhances the book's value. This is such a story. Caspar McCloud shares his journey towards God, and then his journey with God! And from the failures to the triumphs, from the miraculous healings to the agony endured, this story rings true. In the Christian life you don't just 'come to Jesus' and then everything will be all right! Our journey with Jesus is a mirror of His own life on earth; that unless the grain of wheat falls into the ground and dies, it remains alone. Caspar has had to experience this literally to the place of death — only to find that the power of God really is enough. Broadway may be where people first came to hear of Caspar and his role in Beatlemania, but heaven is where the real songs of Caspar's life are going to be sung forever.*"

~ Dr. Tony Dale, Editor
House 2 House magazine

"*The scriptures say that before we were ever born, God knew us. We are wonderfully made and the hand of God is upon us (Psalms 139). That is true as far as God is concerned, but every man and woman has their own journey towards or away from this stated will of God. In Caspar's life his journey began and God was not even in his plans. But God had other plans to preserve his purposes. In time Caspar opened his heart to God but the Devil had his plans to join Caspar in defeating God's will for Caspar's life. In short, two kingdoms clashed, and God and Casper won the battle. I am thrilled to have been part of preserving for God what he has planned in Caspar's life."*

~ Pastor Henry Wright
Pleasant Valley Church

"It has been my privilege the last few years to know Caspar as a friend. I have watched him minister and serve others with sincerity. In "Nothing is Impossible" Caspar articulates well his emotion-filled journey through life. His story offers more than just success and healing but the greater success and victory of making his peace with God through salvation. This book will challenge you to seek the fullness of life and that can only be accomplished by adding God to the picture. It is apparent that God wanted to join Caspar and certainly proved it."

~ Pastor Donna Wright
Pleasant Valley Church

"Caspar Mccloud is a multi-talented artist. He not only makes music with a guitar but with a paint brush as well. His love of horses is evident in his highly rendered and exquisite equestrian paintings that capture every nuance. Caspar inspires people on many levels."

~ Bart Lindstrom
Artist/ Judge and Board member
The Portrait Society of America

NOTHING IS IMPOSSIBLE

Caspar McCloud

With testimonial contributions from
Pastor and author Henry Wright
and medical doctor Terri Allen

Forward by Dove Award–Winning Artist
Phil Keaggy

PRAXIS PRESS
GAINSVILLE, GEORGIA

AUTHOR CONTACT INFORMATION

Pastor Caspar McCloud
In Care of Sanctification Friday's
The Church of the Messiah
415 Charles Cox Drive
Canton, Georgia 30115–4902
Telephone (USA): 770–475–5501

website: www.casparmccloud.com
email: casparmccloud@yahoo.com

Published in Gainesville, Georgia, by
Praxis Press, Inc.
3630 Thompson Bridge Rd., Suite #15-100
Gainesville, GA 30506
www.praxispublishing.com
All Scripture quotations are from the King James Version of the HOLY BIBLE

TO ORDER ADDITIONAL COPIES OF NOTHING IS IMPOSSIBLE
GO TO WWW.CASPARMCCLOUD.COM

Editing Robert Wilson clarifymail@aol.com

Printed in the United States of America.
ISBN-13: 978-0-9754305-4-5
ISBN-10: 0-9754305-4-8

Praises, blessings and thanksgiving be to our Father God, in the name of our Lord Jesus Christ of Nazareth who is able to do (and has done!) exceeding abundantly above all that we could ask or think, according to the power that works in us. Unto him be all the glory!

I also wish to thank my precious wife Joan, our son Derek, and our daughter Hayley for their unending love, and for giving me a taste of heaven on earth.

Acknowledgments

First of all, I want to thank Dr. Terri Allen; of the Fit Center in Montgomery, Alabama; the best physician I have ever known. She is like the Sherlock Holmes of medicine, a brilliant woman of God. I have ministered alongside her and I know first-hand how the Lord uses her to bring healing to this world. I will always remember the profound effect her care has had in my life and I will always be especially grateful for what Dr. Terri said to me at the time my life hung in the balance, "We have tried medicine. Now we must simply just trust in the Lord."

Next, my deepest gratitude goes to my pastors and friends, Donna and Henry Wright. There's nobody like you in the world. You've given me tools and taught me things from the Word that no one else ever showed me—even though these things were there all the time. You met me in my faith--and my faithlessness--and showed me a more excellent way. Thank you for your unending love, boundless faith and availability. God used you to literally give me back my life, and for that, adequate words fail me.

Thank you to Pastor Anita Hill and the entire staff at Pleasant Valley Church. You are more than friends; you are part of my family.

I need to thank Lori Colley who was the first brave soul to edit this work and was a great help in shaping its structure, along with Gary and Jenny Evans, without whose help this book might not have been completed.

I also need to thank Moira French, who serves on staff with me at Sanctification Church and helped with the editing and flow of this manuscript.

I am also deeply grateful to my friend Seth Barnes (the author of "The Art of Listening Prayer") for introducing me to my new friend and our mutual publisher Clint Bokelman. They have both walked along side of me on our journey to share the Gospel, and draw still closer to our Lord continually.

To my friends Matt McCoy and Jim Williams, thank you again for helping with the art work and cover.

I also need to thank my friend Robert Wilson, who did all the final edits on this book and who also experienced a touch from our Lord's healing hand. He is clearly a man who knows how to follow the Lord's instructions and attend to His holy words according to Proverbs 4:20-23.

I pray that all who read this will also apply this truth daily:

My son, attend to my words; incline thine ear unto my sayings. Let them not depart from thine eyes; keep them in the midst of thine heart. For they are life unto those that find them, and health to all their flesh. Keep thy heart with all diligence; for out of it are the issues of life.

Caspar McCloud

Contents

Foreword

I met Caspar McCloud while doing a show in Ohio. He was in a crowd of people but stood out because he looked very British and I could tell, just by looking at him, that he was an artist. He complimented me and asked if we could talk and visit. It was the first of many conversations we were to have over the years.

I shared my faith with him because I sensed in him an earnestness and honesty. He had this longing--perhaps like we all have--a need to be recognized. A pat on the back. Someone to say, "You go for it; you're good." As artists, guitar players and singers we grow up longing for recognition and wanting to be like our heroes in the music world.

Caspar's a really great guitarist with more of the legitimate rock and roll edge that I never had. He seemed like one of the Hollies. I remember praying for him and sharing with him about what God had done in my life. And after that, we just sort of kept in touch long distance. I would encourage him to explore the Bible, to test God, to put his faith in Jesus Christ. It was a long road and there were many turns. Then finally, after about seven years of praying, Caspar showed up backstage at one of my gigs saying, "I really became a Christian. I really gave my life to the Lord!"

And I could just see it! Before for me, it was a matter of encouraging Caspar to believe. But now, I could really see that he had become a Christian. He embraced the faith. He was transformed!

I encourage you to read and believe the amazing story written in these pages. And I hope you will listen to his music. May the Lord use Caspar's message to challenge your beliefs and transform your faith.

Phil Keaggy
Nashville, TN
November 11, 2005

Prologue

The testimony you are about to read is nearly unbelievable because in the natural world what happened to me is not possible. On July 3, 2001, around 9:30 p.m., I collapsed on the floor at Pleasant Valley Church in Thomaston, Georgia. I wasn't breathing. My heart had ceased pumping. I no longer had a pulse. And even with one of the finest physicians in the world at my side, I believe there was nothing medical science could have done to help me.

This is a very real and true account of how the God of the universe, who is the same yesterday, today and forever (Hebrews 13:8), reached down from Heaven to perform a miracle. I am alive and healthier than ever and there is none but the Lord God Almighty to thank. He exchanged a heart filled with disease for a healthy new organ. He exchanged a broken heart for a heart that could truly experience peace, love and joy. To a man who lay on the floor without a heartbeat, he gave brand new life.

Ever since that day I have testified to this miracle—whether it is to someone in the grocery store or to masses of people in a concert audience. I pray that those who are believers in the Lord Jesus Christ will read this and have their own faith increased. And I ask those who are skeptical to read this story with an open mind and heart and just judge for themselves.

Caspar McCloud

The Early Years

To begin explaining my amazing adventure, I will have to go back to the beginnings of my love for art and music. The world of the arts always seemed a backdrop to my life. My parents were classical musicians. I grew up surrounded by their influence and gifted with their genes. I was likewise drawn to painting—fascinated by masters such as Leonardo da Vinci in the way other children are awed by Hall of Fame athletes.

Even at a young age creating masterpieces was my passion. I recall being enrolled in art classes for the gifted when I was very young, and spending my weekends at the art museums instead of playing sports outside like most of my peers. Recognizing the artistic bent of his young son, my father tried to start me on the violin. He was greatly displeased though, when I began strumming, pretending it was a guitar!

My father was very European and my mother was first–generation American. Although I was born in the States, I spent enough time in England over the years to develop a distinctly British manner of speech—and I still sometimes think of England as home. During my childhood we moved a number of times, eventually settling in the North of England (mostly Manchester). Years later we moved to London. Even when I moved to West Palm Beach, Florida with my wife and children in 1988,

I found myself once again among a community of English expatriates. It is true that birds of a feather flock together!

I always remember wanting to do art and music—and to be an equestrian. As a child, it was the only sport I ever cared for. Perhaps my fascination with a fellow who rode a horse and played his guitar explains why the guitar became my instrument of choice. He could have been Roy Rogers, as odd as that may sound, because Roy Rogers was actually a gifted guitarist and singer who rode a palomino named "Trigger," one of the prettiest horses I had ever seen. I still have a passion for horses, and today own and ride a wonderful, magnificent horse named Billy Bob, whom I prefer to introduce as "William Robert", or "Mr. Bob," in polite company.

Actually my black Tennessee Walking Horse looks nothing like Trigger! But I thank the Lord every time I see him waiting for me in our back pasture. Every morning when I go out to feed him, it feels like Christmas.

Disfavored Son

I don't have many good memories of my early years. My family was typically dysfunctional—an unfortunate epidemic running rampant in this present world system. Remember the violin I turned into a guitar? I spent many years trying to gain my father's approval after this fateful incident, but no matter what I did—no matter how many successes I encountered—it never happened. I never heard the words, "I'm proud of you," or "I love you." This lack of reinforcement grieved me deeply for many years. However, I will tell you straight up: I am at peace with it now, as I know my Heavenly Father has given me His approval, and that is all I will ever need.

My parents seemed to argue almost constantly. I recall my mum asking me if she should divorce my father. I was about 4 years old at the time—as if I would know the answer to such a question as that! I am certain I agreed that, yes, she should go through with it. He was such an explosive and emotional fellow I never knew how to read him. One minute he could be jolly, and the next he was on a rampage. I used to hide under my bed when I heard his footsteps, never knowing how he was going to behave. To this day, hearing heavy footsteps coming upstairs releases a cortisol flood (the fight or flight mechanism of the body) into my bloodstream that only the Holy Word of God can stop.

For all I know, my mother told my father about my divorce vote and perhaps he never really forgave me. We had a rather rocky relationship all the years he was alive. Exposed to constant angry voices, I was always looking for a place to escape from the battle lines. I believe that his disdain for me, combined with the rebellion that is "bound up in the heart of a child," led me to my search for identity.

Taking the Reins

Because both my parents worked, I was free to do as I liked much of the time. They let me take riding lessons when I was about 12 years old, and perhaps never knew that jumping was included. That was actually very dangerous behavior back then, since we never wore the head protection that is universally required nowadays—and were riding our mounts over hedges!

I remember the first time my class started to take jumps. I was very fearful that my horse might refuse the jump as I had seen other horses do, with painful results for their riders! My instructor kept pushing me to try. I was the very last rider in my class to go over the jump. (It was intimidating when even the girls in my class had all taken the jump, and I was still trying to avoid it). Finally, I started for the jump in the middle of the arena, putting my horse into a slow canter. Just before we got about a foot away I felt my horse become airborne. It was an amazing sensation! We were actually flying for a brief moment. We hit the ground with such ease I found it incredible that a thousand pound animal could land so gracefully. My instructor gave me the thumbs up. But then he shouted, "Next time keep your eyes open!"

After that first jump, there was no stopping us. I kept galloping back and taking the jumps all over again, loving my newfound freedom. Interestingly, my friend and pastor Henry Wright told me years later that one needs to face his or her fears. Go through them or they will go through you! Once you do, you find freedom on the other side.

I actually got a weekend job in which I would clean fifty stalls in a local horse barn and they let me ride for an hour afterwards as my pay. It seemed a fair exchange at the time. Riding became my great escape; the closest thing I experienced to heaven on earth. There was no strife. There were no problems except an occasional disagreement with my horse, which I usually won.

When I was not riding I fought spirits of depression and loneliness, and found myself drawn to authors like Herman Hess and Thomas Hardy. Their wonderful masterpieces of hardship and tragedy only served to feed my desire to mope about and feel sorry for myself. Today, I recognize that depressive cloud as an unclean spirit of self–pity.

My father wanted to pack me off to a boarding school in London which catered to the arts and took in odd fellows like myself. He thought I was a bit too shy and introverted, and that type of interaction would be good for me. He reckoned that sending me off to school might help bring me out of myself, as it were. But who was I? That was the question I was asking. There was an invisible battle going on for my life between heaven and hell, but I was not able to grasp it at that point.

Flower Power: Sweet and Sour

The "summer of love" occurred during my early teen years, the 1960's. It was a time of incense, peppermints, love beads and "finding yourself." We lived in the States then, and my pals and I were swept up in the British invasion of rock and roll. I embraced it all whole-heartedly. Bands like the Beatles, the Rolling Stones and The Who embodied a style of music that was perfect for a classical music rebel such as me, and I made up my mind to make it my life.

I think that decision was sealed during my early teens when a friend sneaked me into a concert by The Who. We were backstage, two feet away from the legendary Peter Townshend, watching with fascination as he smashed his Stratocaster guitar to bits. Newscasts of the Beatles and the Rolling Stones all showed hordes of pretty girls screaming in adoration, and I'm sure their reaction helped set my course in motion. I remember thinking, "I just want to do that for the rest of my life."

Throughout my teens and into my twenties I wrote songs, played the guitar and sang in bands—the same things I do today. However, back then I was completely consumed by the power of the music. I also worshipped the *gift* of music and not the *Giver*. Practicing guitar endlessly everyday, I often fell asleep with it in my arms. Friends told me that I even played it in my sleep. It became like an extra appendage to my body. This consuming desire drove me to study classical guitar and voice at music conservatories—only because I saw that as a more direct path into the mysteries of the world of music that I found so complex.

Most times I lived very much in my own little world and was quite content to play Bach or lute pieces of the high Renaissance. But sometimes at night, when there was no one there to stop me, instead of practicing pieces from the great masters of classical music, I would play and sing along with one of my favorite albums by Led Zeppelin. I let loose and played and sang the blues from the depth of my soul! I must have been somewhat of an inconsiderate teenager in those times, especially towards my good neighbors. Sometimes late at night, at very inappropriate moments, I would be inspired to experiment and see if I could get my amplifier to feed back as loudly as Jimi Hendrix's!

The world my peers and I were living in was dominated by rebellion growing out of a sense that the whole world was a mess. People were thinking they had missed it somewhere, so they must get back to nature and live in the forest. "Let's change the world," was the maxim of the day. But in the end all I saw was phony inner and outer peace movements and a generation turned off by traditional church, looking for answers in Eastern mysticism.

It is interesting to me that no one ever dared ask, "Why are we listening to some strange Indian on top of a mountain wearing cow dung on his head?" Did we think a fellow like that would have any real answers? Maybe the rock stars, the idols of our time, told us it was so! Upon returning from a trip to India, the Beatles gushed about their new–found guru. He was famous for sayings like, "You feel happiness, you feel peace." And then he would laugh, "He, he, ha, ha," (all the way to the bank with the money he swindled). If he is still living I pray he gets saved in Jesus' name.

I practiced Hinduism for a short time in my teenage years. What did I know? All the guys I looked up to were into this meditation thing. You would sign up as a charter member of the transcendental meditation movement and bring your money and a dozen flowers to your leader, who then started chanting names in another language. As you were led to repeat the name, that became your "mantra." No one told you that you were repeating the name of another god! I had to later repent to the Lord God Almighty for my involvement in this old age/new age lie. I recall I did feel a certain kind of peace when I practiced this false religion. But it was a peace that came at a high price.

We were all just looking for an alternative way to live. People did not want to believe anything from their parents' generation, nor, as the saying goes, trust anyone over thirty. Rebellious spirits were on the loose. And perhaps the church was not equipped to minister to that generation. There are countless stories of hippies being asked to leave a church service because they made the congregation uncomfortable. Pastors like Chuck Smith, who started Calvary Chapel Church and ministry in California, had broken hearts when they saw hippies prevented from attending. Hence, many resigned their powerful positions to start ministries to help get the hippies saved. God blesses that kind of obedience, and today Chuck Smith leads a church of many thousands from all over the U.S.A. I thank the Lord for raising up men like that.

There was also a counter–counter–culture going on populated by "Jesus Freaks." These young people, totally sold out to the Lord, would claim, "Jesus is the answer!" Someone would think it funny to respond, "What's the question?" I thank God that in the midst of my rebellion and idolatry, when religious "freaks" were the butt of my jokes, the Lord had mercy on me and even then had a plan for my life.

Trip to Nowhere

I had a few good friends who put up with me being the temper-amental artist type. They were good students and good kids, but eventually we all got caught up in the end of the hippie drug age and experimented. I held out longer than most. I would pretend to smoke whatever my friends handed me. Only I never inhaled, I just squeezed the end so hard that nothing would come out! I tried to just fit in, but never quite did.

I had a friend who was an excellent guitarist and I greatly admired him and his talented family. He and his brothers toured at times with hit musicals like "Godspell," and he would sometimes get to jam with a number of rock stars. One day, when I was about 15 years old, he convinced me that if I smoked hashish with him I would learn to play better—that it would free my spirit and give my spirit energy. Right! My other friend, who was also an artist I greatly admired, said it would help me paint even better. I finally gave in, and it all went terribly wrong. I ended up at a clinic on a bad trip, thinking I was dead. If I had problems before, experimenting with mind–altering drugs only made things much worse.

I suffered from frequent flashbacks, reliving the horror of that trip. My friend's parents, Pete and Heidi, took me in, nursed me until I came back to reality, and let me live with them from time to time after that. They were the only parents I'd ever met who really loved each other and I became quite dependent on them for all kinds of advice. No matter how bad things got in my life, they always helped me see a rainbow at the end of the storm.

One day, I asked Heidi why they were so kind to me, and she told me the story of the Good Samaritan. They were kind to all of us teenagers. It was common to go to their home where the music of the Byrds played in the background and teenagers filled every available space. We were eight miles high as a normal, everyday experience. Pete and Heidi made their home a refuge, a place where we could be safe from the outside world, but where they could keep an eye on us. Little did I know that the real danger came from an invisible spirit world that wanted to keep us from knowing the truth.

Pete and Heidi did not have all the answers, however much I loved them. They attended a church that was hardly a church at all, but a place to drink tea and coffee and chat. I concluded it was for people who were raised to go to church, but who were now in rebellion and just wanted a place to go on Sunday morning. They believed in God, but weren't sure who he was.

I went to their church for a while, but it still did not fill the void in my heart. People there were as strange and mixed up as I was. And I was rather strange at times, to put it mildly! Many of my artist friends would spend time at Pete and Heidi's home. It seemed we were all into surrealism and it penetrated our everyday view of reality.

I kept asking questions and searching for truth in all of this. Even though I had friends who really loved me now, it still wasn't enough; something was missing in my life.

I was curious about the man from the past who was called Jesus Christ of Nazareth and claimed to be the Son of God. Somewhere along the way I read a story about the shroud of Turin, and concluded that this Jesus Christ of Nazareth was real. But I was not yet ready to surrender to Him. I was having too much fun! (Much later, after I became a Christian, I ended up recording a song on my first Christian album entitled, "I'm Having More Fun Going to Heaven than I Ever Had Going to Hell.")

A Divine Appointment

I was awarded a scholarship to an art and music college in Cleveland, Ohio and started playing in clubs on the weekends. One night I was auditioning for a band in front of a live audience at a pub, and a fellow came up to me and started to offer me a management contract. He told me I was the best thing he had heard since Christian guitarist Phil Keaggy. Well, it turned out that he was Phil Keaggy's old manager—the one who managed Phil's band, "Glass Harp." Phil had recently left the band and this man apparently had a plan to keep things going with me.

A friend at school told me she knew Phil and his wife Bernadette. She suggested I find out why he left the band before I signed my life away. She arranged for us to have dinner with the Keaggys that weekend. We had a wonderful evening together and Phil shared his faith with me. One of the most profound scriptures he quoted was Psalm 33:3, "Play skillfully with a loud noise." Now, coming from parents who played classical music, and coming at a time when organized religion rejected anything remotely "loud," it just stunned me. How could something that had been written in the Bible thousands of years ago be so applicable in my life today?

I had never before met anyone like Phil. It really did not matter to me then, nor does it matter to me now, that Phil is such a brilliant musician. He won me over with the love of God. I could tell Phil and Bernadette genuinely cared for me. There was such love and concern in Phil's eyes that sometimes I felt as though it was really the Lord Jesus looking through him at me. Often Phil would quote something from the Bible which made me feel uncomfortable because I was living in a way that didn't line up with what it said. I really wanted to know how Phil and his wife knew God personally! But when I would leave them, the world would grab at me once again with all its empty promises of fame and fortune, and I would be lost and lonely again. What a blessing to have the Keaggys befriend me at that time! In those days I struggled with suicidal thoughts because I did not understand much about spiritual warfare and the importance of bringing every thought into captivity to the obedience of Christ (II Corinthians 10:5).

Of Three Minds

I have learned that thoughts originate from one of three places. They are either genuinely your own, such as, "Boy, I'm hungry" when your stomach growls, or they can come from somewhere else. If you are a believer you have the Spirit of God and the thought can come from him who dwells within you. This is the still small voice of your conscience. Then there is a third source for thoughts: the enemy, Satan, and his army of evil spirits.

Few people realize that there must be a being to think a thought! In Genesis, God asked Adam, "Who <u>told</u> you that you were naked?" The thought couldn't have originated with Adam because he was unaware of the whole concept of clothes. And it certainly didn't come from God. I believe that the thoughts of guilt and shame that accompanied Adam's sin came from Satan because they caused Adam to run *from* God, rather than *to* Him in repentance.

Even today, the Bible says, Satan roams about like a roaring lion, seeking whom he may devour. Does he physically eat us alive? No! He attacks us in our thoughts, because "as a man thinketh, so is he." That is why we need to take our thoughts captive; if they don't measure up to the Word of God, we need to cast them out. Disallow them! Pay them no heed! Satan wants to hold us captive through guilt and shame and fear, but the Holy Spirit gently leads us into repentance and restoration.

Before I was a believer, I remember thinking that if I ever really got into trouble, Phil would be the first person I would call. He would write me from the road, his letters salted with Bible verses. He'd call me on the phone and hit me with Scripture, and I would think, "Why can't he just speak English?" Since I was still resisting, the Word of God made little sense to me. Yet, all that time, Phil kept bringing my name before the Father. I know now that God watches over his Word to perform it, and his Word does not come back to him void.

I will be forever grateful to Phil for his faithfulness because after years of searching, I finally surrendered my life to Christ Jesus the Lord—but not before I began looking into the occult. Phil warned me against it, but I recall thinking he just didn't understand this intellectual world. He understood it much better than I knew, and I should have heeded his warning! I know now that this attraction to the occult wasn't even my own thoughts, but evil spirits who were assigned to try and pull me into deception.

Ungodly Music

I was trying to finish my degree but kept dropping out to play in bands that were hoping to accomplish something important—whatever that was! We were so idealistic in those days. Music can be a very powerful emotional trigger that can even change your body's chemistry and cause you to feel many things—some that you may not want to confront.

Let me please warn you to be careful what you listen to and take into your spirit and soul! The devil—who was called Lucifer before he was expelled from Heaven—was in charge of music before his fall (Ezek. 28:13). Pastor Henry Wright once told me that sanctification of music comes from the words behind it or the spirit behind it (if an instrumental). This gives one tremendous freedom in the form and shape the music may take. Relax! You do not have to listen only to the most popular and latest recorded music from Nashville. But, praise to God, you are free to worship as the Holy Spirit leads you—whether that sounds like Bach, Beethoven, an Indian raga, some heavy metal band or anything in–between.

For those of you who prefer music sung by Doris Day or Julie Andrews or music that sounds like sugar and honey dripping together, be my guest. Please take your freedom, and please allow the rest of us ours.

The Sins of Youth

My life continued in a somewhat disjointed fashion for some time. I never did finish college, but played in bands and kept my relationship with Pete and Heidi. Then finally, in 1975, I enrolled in Case Western Reserve College in Cleveland, Ohio.

Although I lived in Ohio, I was hanging out with two English friends named Lawrence and John. Both were very charming fellows, and more than reasonably intelligent. John's father was a noted British scientist who had a number of appointments over the years from Her Majesty Queen Elizabeth II. Lawrence had a penchant for traveling the world. Together, these two were always looking for pretty young ladies to chat up.

I was their Bohemian artist friend who had almost emigrated to New Zealand the previous year to be with a girl I'd taken a fancy to named Jennifer. Her parents were prominent members of New Zealand society and such was their influence that they successfully deterred me from absconding with their daughter. Did you know that English towns used to lock the city gates at night to protect their women and virgins by keeping the musicians out? Her parents may have been thinking that a few gates and moats would have come in handy when I was chasing Jennifer. Of course, I was ignorant of the Bible in those days and was not yet a believer. I paid a very high price for my ignorance and later had to ask the Lord to forgive my transgressions against him and others.

Have you ever thought about how many sins you have unknowingly committed? Can you remember a time when you repented of them? Even believers fall into sins they have not discerned, and few people realize how much we also struggle with the effects of the iniquities of our ancestors (Num. 14:18). Yet we wonder why our prayers go answered! It is so vital to know the Word of God! We must spend time with other believers who can speak the truth in love and point us back to the right path when we wander off. When we willfully sin as believers, we crucify the Lord all over again. We give the enemy a place and a legal right to come and interfere with our health, emotions and spirit.

Behold, the Lord's hand is not shortened, that it cannot save: neither His ear heavy that it cannot hear: But your iniquities have separated between you and your God, and your sins have hid His face from you, that He will not hear. (Isaiah 59:1–2)

These verses say that God will not hear but that is not something I hear taught very often in the churches. No wonder the church looks so much like the world. A Scottish minister friend of mine named Bob Evans will often ask a congregation, "Is the church today impacting the world, or is the world impacting the church?" What do you think? What do you see happening? Are you more attracted to the world—or the things of the Spirit? Are you more interested in watching television and movies than reading your Bible? Are the films and television shows God–centered or world–centered? Which type of films do you prefer to watch? Do you ever find that the shows you watch have taught you something you later regretted learning?

It's so easy to fall into sin; it's so easy to follow the crowd. It's so easy to offend someone or let yourself be offended. It's so easy to follow the world's way into pride and lying and greed. But please ask yourself one question now, "How can a holy God bless me in my sin?

Your iniquities have turned away these things, and your sins have withholden good things from you. (Jeremiah 5:25)

My people are destroyed for lack of knowledge: because thou hast rejected knowledge, I will also reject thee, that thou shall be no priest to Me: seeing thou hast forgot the law of thy God, I will also forget thy children. (Hosea 4:6)

If I regard iniquity in my heart, the Lord will not hear me... (Psalm 66:18)

The sins of my youth had begun to affect my body. I had given place to the fear I felt as a child and developed very bad allergies. Do you know that allergies result from a breakdown in the immune system? The body releases cortisol when it finds itself in a fearful situation. Well, I had grown up in fear—living in a dysfunctional home where one never knew when the other shoe would drop. That constant state of fear and the continual drip of cortisol in my body wore out my immune system, so that I could no longer tolerate dust, pet dander and certain foods. In addition, I also had a broken heart from being rejected by my father, which shattered my peace and gave place to spirits of self–pity. This is how my heart began to be so full of disease.

The Bible says that the iniquities of the fathers are passed on to the third and fourth generations (Deut. 5:9) until someone learns how to break the power of these sin–propelled curses. It would have cost me my life, had it not been for the promises and provisions of the Lord I discovered by studying under the ministry at Pleasant Valley Church. I never realized until I became a believer and learned how my dabbling in the occult hurt God's heart, that I had also unwittingly opened my own spirit up to all sorts of demonic influences.

Art School Escapades

I was studying parapsychology while in art school at Case Western because, believe it or not, art school actually demands that you get a proper education. We were required to study English, history, mathematics, etc., so one could not just draw and paint all day, or ride a horse on the equestrian team! While studying parapsychology, I became completely caught up in learning about invisible powers, and I considered leaving art to become a psychology major. Fortunately, one of my favorite college professors, Dr. Kirk Wheeler, convinced me it was obvious I was meant to pursue the arts.

Dr. Wheeler is a very brilliant man and I greatly admired him. He let me enroll in a doctorate–level psychic phenomena class. Trying to convince these highly educated classmates of my superior understanding of life, I showed up for the first day of class wearing white–face and a cape, wielding a real sword. It had wonderful shock value with all those serious doctoral students! Another pursuit I enjoyed, ever seeking to prove I was the eccentric artist, was riding my horse in full medieval garb through the countryside like a knight from the Middle Ages.

Artist Salvador Dali (of the dripping clocks) was another one of my heroes. I figured that the more eccentric I acted, the more successful I would eventually become. After all, it had worked for Dali! Some time after I left the college, I met one of my former instructors who said he did not recognize me without the white face and costumes. This behavior won me much popularity with the student art world, bent as they were on shock value. It was a time when artists and art critics began to proclaim that bizarre images of self–mutilation or human excrement were things of supreme value. Who do you think was inspiring these sorts of artistic visions?

I did not like these "cutting–edge" images even then. My passion was to paint as convincingly as possible. The other genre seemed like the townsfolk in Hans Christian Anderson's tale of "The Emperor's New Clothes." Often the work lacking in artistic value is the one that's highly praised. The "intelligent ones" in artistic circles claim that the only thing preventing the rest of the world from appreciating shocking art is our stupidity and lack of vision.

The last day of the psychic phenomena class we held a sort of psychic party, which involved playing with Ouija boards. What I did not understand at the time was that we had invited an evil spirit in to answer our questions. This spirit (also called a familiar spirit) can impersonate the deceased.

Regard not them that have familiar spirits, neither seek after wizards, to be defiled by them: I am the Lord your God. (Leviticus :31)

A couple of years later I enrolled in art school in England. Some of my mates, who were also interested in these subjects, would join me on the weekends to visit a known haunted castle or stay up all night in the woods by a river and watch the sky for a UFO. In our ignorance, we were captivated by the occult.

Our main hobby was getting into trouble. Just before exams one year, my friend Marc convinced a young female model to pose for us back at his flat. Marc had a room in a mansion, on loan from a wealthy family who wanted to support his art. There were several empty servants' rooms next to the ballroom. So Marc proposed that we get an advantage on our upcoming life–drawing exams by having this model pose nude in the ballroom.

There were five of us drawing that Saturday afternoon. Our model was a professional who knew us well from art school. We all spent the time doing what we were supposed to be doing, drawing her. She knew we were serious artists and she felt safe with us. Just as medical students have to know the human anatomy, so do art students. We had to learn and draw all the bones, muscles and flesh. So, as odd as this must sound, we were serious art students trying to make good grades.

Later that day, being gentlemen, we escorted her to the back door of the estate.

Marc must have known there was a very posh tea party going on and marched us all through the midst of it. Then, at a moment when every eye was upon us, he reached in his pocket to give our lovely young model a fist full of cash, and said, "Here you are love, you were really great!" A few teacups dropped to the floor that day!

On a subsequent Friday I had another class painting a nude model. She was another pretty female model, but I treated her as I did all models; just as though she was a bowl of fruit. Nearly finished with my painting, I did not want to stop when the others broke for tea. She saw me working and came over to say that I had done such a splendid job painting her, why didn't I just come over to her place to finish up?

Fantastic! I thought, and told my professor who agreed to come along with me. We arrived at her flat and I knocked on the door. The smile on her face turned to one of distress as she noticed my professor standing there with me. Suddenly, she had come down with a bad headache. I never could understand why she was so upset with me after that.

Phil Keaggy always told me that I was too childlike and naïve about things in this world. From time to time he felt he needed to protect me. But he said my naiveté was also a blessing because it also meant I had a childlike faith in God after I got saved. I can still believe the Lord for just about anything.

That innocence almost took my life on a different track. Even though I always wanted to be an artist/musician, I got the idea of becoming a medical illustrator and so enrolled in medical school. On the first day I was to draw in the cadaver class. Rather than being repulsed, I was excited; having read how my hero Leonardo da Vinci used to study cadavers. However, when I opened the door to the room, got a whiff of the formaldehyde, and saw doctors at work on actual dead bodies, I quickly closed the big swinging door and for once did a sensible thing. I ran away!

It just so happened that the head of the New Zealand National Art Museum was visiting the art school, and had asked me to sing and play a song I had written for a video they were filming. Because it was scheduled for the same day as the cadaver class, I told him I could not do it because of a conflict. But after escaping the dead bodies, I remembered the filming and ran to the museum office. Fortunately, they still needed me. As soon as I got in front of the film crew I knew I was where I needed to be. I now understand that God has a plan and a purpose for each of us and it is so important to find and do what we are created to do.

The Love of My Life

In particular, God's plan for me had included college in Ohio at Case Western, which permitted a chance meeting I could easily have missed. One day John and Lawrence came round to my room and asked me to go out with them on New Year's Eve. I said, "No, I don't want to see anyone or meet anyone. You fellows go without me and have a good time." (I probably looked out a window and held my hand to my head in some exaggerated pose.) They insisted I come anyway, knowing that I was still depressed over the recent ending of my relationship with Jennifer, the girl from New Zealand. My pattern was always the same whenever self–pity and perfectionism flooded my thoughts. I would just work on a painting all night and then destroy it, claiming the work was not good enough.

So off we went to pub after pub, the same routine as always. I would sit and watch them pick up young ladies—or watch them strike out. Even when they did start a relationship, it didn't seem to last very long. A few days, a week or two and they would fancy someone else. No one seemed to really want lasting relationships in those days. There was a saying: "Love them and leave them." I think that fellow Stephen Stills who sang "Love the One You're With," summed up the heart of that generation.

I didn't want to play that game—I longed for something else. I was nursing my broken heart and pining away for a lost romance that was more infatuation, perhaps, than love. I did not really know of many married couples who seemed to have a wonderful ongoing relationship anyway. Da Vinci never married, so maybe that was how to accomplish something great, since there were no distractions. I once heard someone say that a good woman can cause a man to do great things, but the wrong one can prevent him from accomplishing anything.

20

So I was not about to play the dating game. Sometimes I thought about being a monk so no one could ever hurt me again. The only problem was that I hadn't heard of many monks playing in rock bands or riding horses! I would keep myself entertained by these dejected thoughts until I saw a pretty girl go by. Then I would realize that being a monk was not such a good idea after all.

Finally, I got fed up with the whole thing and, sitting there with John and Lawrence that New Year's Eve, I decided I would see how many girls I could charm into going out with me. "I'll show you how it should be done. Just watch me, fellows, and do what I do!"

I began working on the ladies, charming them left and right like birds out of the trees. Soon I had found that I had collected an assortment of telephone numbers. I was on a roll! (Keep in mind how many hurting people are out there still just waiting for anyone to notice them.) I had found the secret to this dating thing. You had to actually go after a girl you were interested in and say something. Almost any line would work, as long as you were honest. Most people are so afraid of being rejected they won't say a word.

That was when I met Joan, the most beautiful woman I had ever seen. She was also intelligent and witty—a dream come true. The more I tried to get her to notice me the more she ignored me. (She later told me she did that on purpose.) I even started telling her stories about how I knew all these famous rock stars, and I was going to be one someday. Even though it was the truth, she thought I was making it all up. All the other girls started surrounding me and I was trying to escape them all and go after Joan. Finally I got to talk with her, and I could tell she liked me as well.

As I was leaving I gave her a kiss, which she accepted. It was the most wonderful kiss I ever had before; one that I will always remember, where you hear romantic music start to play and rockets blast off in the background. I even told her right then that she was the most beautiful woman I'd ever seen. And would she marry me, as I needed a wife to carry my guitar? It was a line I must have stolen from a Groucho Marx film.

It was later, standing outside, that I learned she was Lawrence's girlfriend! John, Lawrence and I were standing under a street light with the winter snow softly collecting on our faces. I knew Lawrence was not serious about her. So I asked him if I could ask her out—as if it would have made a difference! At the same time I handed him all the telephone numbers I had collected that evening with great confidence saying, "Here, mate. I won't be needing these anymore!"

Bad Movie, Burned Tongue

I took the liberty of memorizing Joan's telephone number when I was at the New Year's Eve party. I rang her up the next day and asked her out, and we have been together ever since! That was 1977.

Our first date was to go see a play about a deranged teenage boy who set a barn on fire and then blinded a stable full of racehorses. It was Joan's idea, and not her best decision! But we didn't give up. For our second date she decided she'd make me a lovely Mexican dinner. I, accustomed to English cooking, took one bite and went running to the kitchen faucet because my mouth was on fire! How was I to know they put hot sauce on that stuff?

Joan remembers that I asked her to see my etchings. Being an artist, I really did have etchings! It was a good pick–up line so I used it with her. I had her pose for a painting of a left–handed cellist. Remember that rebellious spirit? I got to thinking, why does everyone in the orchestra have to play right–handed? If I had given it any thought, I would have realized how many bowed instruments would have clashed like a sword fight, sitting next to each other.

I painted Joan every chance I got. One winter day I surprised her with a request to pose outside in the woods. Unfortunately, that day she had dressed to please me, and wore a lovely long Victorian skirt with summer–type footwear. After a while she began fighting frostbite. I think I realized then that she would do just about anything for me.

As time went on, Joan told me about her alcoholic father who had gone on a rage one day. He shot Joan's mother to death in front of her and her brothers and sisters. Then he put the gun to his own head and shot himself. She was only thirteen years old. My heart went out to her. We were two hurting people looking for love and someone to care for us. I recall thinking I must be there for her, I must protect her, and I must have her.

What I have learned since then is that the issues that cripple us are often the things that draw people together. We both had spirits of rejection and broken hearts, and neither of us had been healed emotionally or spiritually. Does this mean our marriage—or any similar marriage—was wrong? Absolutely not! But it does mean we had a lot of stuff to work through, and I praise God that we have each received deliverance and healing.

You see, I was so naive about this whole grown–up kind of love. I bought Joan an engagement ring (that she helped pick out). We had a picnic in the woods and I took the wrong hand; I really did not even know what hand the ring went on back then. Joan kept pulling her hand away and gently gave me her left hand. And that was that.

We were married six months later. I grabbed my good friend Howard Wallach, an accomplished classical guitarist who has since published many wonderful books for the guitar, and asked him to be our witness. It was a last minute thing: one day we just got up and saw that the sun had come out and thought it would be a good day to get married! We had been living together for six months and needed to make it official straightway due to some documents which would affect out taxes.

After the courthouse wedding, we went out and ordered wedding rings. When they arrived a week later, we amazed the jeweler by putting both on and proceeding to walk out of his shop. He mentioned that most people wait until the wedding to put rings on. We just giggled and kept going.

Years later, I found myself repenting to the Lord for the way our marriage started out, and for living together before we were married. It is not God's way and I would strongly urge anyone going that direction to get back on the path to holiness straightway. We acted out of rebellion and ignorance—two things the devil loves to work with. You need to do things God's way if you want his holy protection and blessing.

Soon I was offered an automatic Bachelor of Fine Arts degree from an art college if I would just spend a year and finish my Master's degree there. It seemed like a wonderful opportunity, and it was. They thought I was such a brilliant artist. They would have offered me the moon if it was theirs to give. All I had to do was take a few classes, write a few papers and paint paintings all year. Instead, I chose to go to Broadway, thinking I could always do my degree later. Honestly, how many chances does one get to be in a hit musical?

So let me share that part of my life with you, as it all has a purpose. I am trying to be as transparent as I can, and let you know the good bits and the difficult times I encountered along the way.

Beatles and Broadway

One day I went to the Salvador Dali museum and met the coordinator. We ended up becoming friendly and she offered to introduce me to Mr. and Mrs. Morris, owners of the Dali Collection. On the day we had arranged to meet, I waited in an outside office and Mrs. Morris came bursting into the room. She extended her hand and said, "You're British aren't you? I can tell simply by your brush strokes!"

She then told me that if she and her husband did not already patronize Mr. Dali, they would have liked to patronize me. What an amazing compliment! Mrs. Morris then arranged for me to meet Mr. Dali at the St. Regis Hotel in New York. But when I arrived in New York, my meeting was postponed as he had come down with a case of the flu. I did speak with him for a few minutes on the hotel telephone. It was a very surreal conversation, and to this day none of it makes any sense. But my date with Mr. Dali was never to take place because a date with Broadway intervened.

It was back in the late 70's, and I was living in the eastern part of the U.S. Every person in my circle of friends was talking about the new production of Beatlemania and the auditions that were being held. My friend Mickey tried to convince me to go out for a part. I thought it was a daft idea! I didn't even really look like any of the Beatles. In fact, I was told I looked like all of the Beatles put together. Did that include Ringo? (No offense, mate!) Although I had the right accent, I didn't think I was right for any of the parts.

Mickey had me watch a movie entitled "The Rutles," a satire from the Monty Python comedy troupe. Somehow Eric Idle was so convincing as a Paul McCartney–type that I was beginning to believe I might have a chance at this Broadway production after all. Mickey had a friend who did lighting for the show and so I was able to secure an audition through him.

I had done a little bit of acting in college the year before and I thought I might be able to swing it. However, when I arrived for the audition, the only part they hadn't yet cast was for John Lennon. At that point, I was so caught up in the possibilities, I thought, "Yeah, I can do Lennon—I can be sensitive and nasty at the same time!"

Amazingly, this was not my first encounter with rock stars and fame. One of my very best friends at art school, David Kirk, along with his brother Dan, introduced me to Peter Gabriel, who was the lead singer in Genesis, then a very successful band in the United Kingdom. David had told Peter that I was the best guitarist he had ever heard. Mind you, we were just out of our teens and so we had not really heard all that much yet! But David was one of my biggest supporters. Where my earthly father had programmed me to think I could not accomplish what I wanted to do, David kept reprogramming me, telling me that I <u>could</u> do it.

David took me to see his friend Peter Gabriel several times. Peter was very kind to me and invited me to his home. In the course of our conversations he began preparing me for future auditions, and introducing me to the fascinating world of show business.

David and Dan Kirk were also the ones who really helped me develop my approach to painting. David and I were in art school together and we were both attracted to the Pre–Raphaelites and spent time in England studying the various museum collections. Dan started doing cover illustrations for major magazines like *Time* and *Newsweek*, while David developed a line of artistic toys that made him some sort of cult hero before he found his niche as a best–selling author/illustrator of children's books. We all sort of helped each other where we could. I would sometimes paint sections of the toys David invented, while Joan would pose for some assignment Dan was illustrating. Both David and Dan would critique my latest artwork—which always propelled me to do even better.

There was an underlying competitive edge that would come out when we played Scrabble together. You had to come up with impressive words, not just words to gain points. But at the same time we were like family and rejoiced in each other's successes.

Dan had an artist's loft across from the water on the south side of Manhattan. There were tall ships across the street and also a large fish market below us. I can still smell those fish! The brothers had moved in together for a season, so they graciously let me stay there whilst I was seeking my big audition. I would practice all the Beatles' songs in their bathroom, knowing they were probably laughing their heads off at me.

Mickey's friend was able to help me get a private audition with the director, and learn what songs to perform to give them what they wanted. Finally the day arrived for the audition at SIR Studios. I got dressed like a Beatle and went to meet the director.

Instead of impressing the boss, I was made fun of by many in the cast. I waited there all day long in my rather hot black Beatles suit. It was summer and this was New York City—the town without pity. The director left messages for me all day that he would be there soon, but he never showed up.

This went on all week. I'd get there early dressed as a Beatle with stage makeup on, etc., and wait while most of the cast made me the brunt of their jokes.

The hardest part was riding the subways dressed in full Beatle garb. But since it was New York City no one really cared or took any notice, except for tourists who stared relentlessly! By Thursday, it was time for open auditions. A cattle call for me and about 3,000 other hopefuls. When it was my turn to audition, I was asked to sing and play guitar. I remember being incredibly confident taking on the character of Lennon. I was built for this part, I thought.

The director kept his eyes on me, and finally said, "You're the one who waited all week for me?" Then he pointed me out in the crowd and said, "Can you do, 'Help'?" He was looking for someone as aggressive as I was being. When I was about half way through the first verse of the song, he stopped me and said, "You. You're it." And so I was cast as John Lennon in Beatlemania.

Then, as an after–thought, the director said, "Wait. Can you play keyboard?" Feeling slightly shook up, I somehow managed to play an arpeggio (which made me look like I knew what I was doing), and then proceeded to play, "I am the Walrus." Apparently, this confirmed his decision.

In less than a minute I went from nobody special to rising star on Broadway. My life was about to take a turn into what many people would consider a dream come true. Playing on stage in front of screaming fans. Basking in the bright lights and thunderous applause. Life shifted into high gear.

Sometime later I was at a party with my pals Dan and David, who began introducing me as their friend, the "rock star." It was the first time I realized that my dreams were actually coming true. Even though I did not really feel like a star, people were treating me like one.

For six months I played the part, immersed in the world of Broadway. Meeting fascinating people. Sharing rehearsal floors with bands like the Rolling Stones. Jamming and making friends with famous musicians. One such person, who had performed at Woodstock, was a huge influence in my burgeoning Broadway career. He produced my first real studio recording at Jimi Hendrix's Electric Ladyland in Greenwich Village. I even got to play and record with some of Hendrix's old amplifiers.

My new mate gathered a number of rock stars to help with my recording. Unfortunately, most of them were high on drugs and we recorded the rhythm parts so fast that I could hardly sing over it at the vocal session. Later on, while we were at some late night rock star party, this friend told me I was too talented to be wasting my career being a "fake Beatle."

Sad Saga of Starting Over

Little did I know that he would soon talk me into ending my Broadway career for good. You would think that the fame and fortune—more money than I had ever made before—would have kept me there. But once again, I was very naive and trusted other people's opinions. I figured that because they'd been around, they must know what was best. Well, this musician I refer to, a member of a very prestigious band that is still going strong today, appealed to my ego. He went on and on about my talent and potential. He listed the possibilities of taking the stage on my own. And before long, he had me believing that the real stuff wasn't on Broadway; "real" was a solo gig. Finally, I agreed with him. I resigned my role as John Lennon and went out on my own. I should have taken just a moment to consider that my buddy was smoking a joint at the time he gave me all this great advice.

Joan and I found ourselves homeless, jobless and back in England. Thus began a season of frustration. The "glamorous solo life" consisted of playing for a handful of people in a smoke–filled pub, being paid barely enough to buy a bag of fish and chips. Even when things got a bit better and I did join a band with better gigs and more steady income it wasn't what I'd hoped for. As the opening act for other bands, our celebrity was next to nothing, and so was our pay.

But I plugged along. At one point I received news that EMI Records from London were interested in a record deal. The night I received the news, we were to follow the opening act, Mr. Ray and the Angels.

They were a transvestite group. England can be a very strange place at times—nothing odd here, just good old British entertainment! The pub was in the Great Western Hotel in Manchester, and the owner let us practice there as long as we played for free once a week. Need I say I was not exactly surrounded by a bunch of wholesome Christians? But these were my fans, some of whom really seemed to love us, between their drinks.

The next night, EMI was out there listening to us. Everything was going very well. The crowd was as thick as the smoke in the air and a feeling of excitement permeated the room. News had gotten around that guys from the A & R (Artist & Repertoire) department of a big–name record company were coming up from London to listen to my band. When I walked out onto the stage that night the place just exploded with applause. The band played like a machine that would rock the walls down, and the louder we got the more the people cheered.

I noticed something out of the corner of my eye, but I just kept playing. I could see the record company executives were enjoying our act. In fact, they were giving me a "thumbs–up." Then suddenly, a fight broke out. Some sailors had been hitting on a very pretty woman sitting at a table. One grabbed her hair as if he were a cave man. Immediately, a very well dressed young man, who actually looked like he might have been a librarian, came to her rescue. He said very gallantly to the attackers, "Unhand that damsel, you ruffians!"

For that very courageous act, the sailor punched the librarian in the nose and knocked him out cold. Within seconds, the whole place erupted into one big brawl—just like an old cowboy movie, with people swinging from chandeliers and bottles flying across the bar and smashing against the mirror.

My mate Russ, who played guitar and sang harmony with me, ended up stuffed into the bass drum. He was in too much pain to carry on when the dust settled. The drummer was all banged up as well. The EMI representatives told me that they really liked the band but didn't get a chance to hear enough, since all this happened during the second song. They exclaimed it was a pity it ended on such a rough note, and perhaps when the band recovered they would come listen again. And with that, they left. I went home very depressed.

But soon another promising possibility surfaced in the form of Michael Ward, the road manager for a band called Mink Deville. He had connections and offered to manage my career. Off I went to London to make a demo in which both Virgin Records and EMI expressed interest. Michael called me up absolutely thrilled. "Richard Branson from Virgin Records is sending a limo for you!" Joan insisted I wear a coat and tie. Michael and I were wined and dined at the fanciest, most expensive restaurant I had ever seen.

Playing Hard to Get

Our conversation that night was moving along nicely toward a deal, but at the same time it was like playing poker. We didn't want to appear too eager, yet I was anxious for that contract. One of their executives (they seem to travel in schools, like fish) began to denigrate my potential. He voiced his opinion that maybe at 25, I was too old! Shouldn't I have made the big time already? Maybe my best days had passed.

Time for me to play my hand. "All right," I offered, "I'll be glad to leave right now and call EMI first thing in the morning." And so I got up from the table and began leaving the room. They panicked and ran after me, apologizing profusely. We took the limo back to their office, and that night the contract was arranged.

Why was I so anxious to cement this deal with Virgin? I had been around and seen how the other companies functioned. At one record label, I was taken into Rod Stewart's office. It was quite opulent: an obscenely thick white carpet covered the floor and everything in the office was white or gold. Looking upon one wall, I saw a portrait of Stewart. He was wearing a kilt and had his arm around a lion. This type of window dressing was typical for most labels. But Virgin was different. There, I got the sense of real people working real jobs, with none of the fancy stuff. Messy desks, lots of offices, working class; I felt right at home.

I was satisfied with the offer from Virgin. But Joan and Michael both thought it was too much of me for too little from them. They convinced me I needed to wait for a better deal, and it became one of those decisions I regretted for years and years. I reluctantly agreed to get a lawyer to help me lobby for more money and contacted a friend from the band Santana who sent me to his lawyer.

Right in the midst of these negotiations, I got a call from my father saying that my mother was very ill. She had cancer and it didn't look like she would live more than a few days. He urged me not to go back to Ohio because he didn't want to see me again. But the emotional pressure to see her was enormous.

Joan and I were flat broke, and selling one of my best guitars was the only way I could afford to purchase a plane ticket. So I left the contract negotiations in the hands of the lawyer I had engaged, packed a few things, and boarded a plane for the States. Thankfully, I was able to spend more than a few days with my mum, as she battled on for a couple more months. It was a very difficult time and to make matters worse, I was completely broke and very anxious about the Virgin deal.

And so I should have been. Receiving a phone call, I learned some terrible news. Virgin executives were fed up with my lawyer. They said they couldn't work with him anymore and with me not there to smooth things out, everything fell apart.

By this time my mother was gone, I was emotionally battling my father's rejection, and there I was with no money, half a world away from where I wanted to be and swimming in a sea of self–pity. Did I mourn my mother's passing? Yes. But I wasn't able to grieve properly, or show any emotion. I had turned into a performer; I had taken on the rough nasty character flaws of the Lennon I once played. I felt hopeless.

Little did I know that while all of this was happening, Michael Ward had succeeded in getting me a deal with EMI back in London. He phoned me in Ohio, but I was so despondent I wouldn't take the call. Having no money and no advances, I was stuck; eventually taking a job in a record store. I really had no experience in retail, but the owner felt sorry for me. I was managing all right until a certain stage production came to town called Beatlemania. The news pierced my heart. If it's possible, I became even more depressed.

Day of Salvation

In the meantime, my marriage was in trouble—mostly because I wasn't there. Although Joan understood that I needed to be gone most of the time, deep down she was still hurting from her difficult childhood. Even though we had been reunited in Ohio, I was not home very often to support her. One day it got so bad that she left and flew to be with her sisters in Fort Wayne, Indiana. I was devastated and began entertaining suicidal thoughts again. Woe is me! Could life get any worse?

Meanwhile, a deal was cooking in New York City that needed my attention. A record company was interested in signing me. It was enough of a jolt that I decided that before I took my life, I would get on a plane and apologize to Joan for being such a beastly, self–centered, poor excuse of a husband.

My good friend David Kirk helped me get to the airport, where I found myself sprinting through the terminal trying to catch the flight. I remember running with my guitar and a shoulder bag, but I could not run fast enough, so I just dropped them. I made the airplane in time and they let me board. I just had to see Joan once more and tell her that I was very sorry for causing her so much pain. It was winter, and I reckoned that after I told her how sorry I was, I would simply disappear into a nearby forest and lie down and die. No one would even find me until the spring. Where were all these thoughts coming from? Surely not from the Lord!

During the flight, thousands of feet in the air, I started remembering years of Holy Scripture that Phil Keaggy had shared with me. It never made much sense until this moment, at this time in my life. Flying close to heaven, looking out my window and seeing we were above the clouds, the truth was abundantly clear. I now knew whom I needed and cried out to God. I recall praying something like this:

> Jesus Christ of the Holy Bible, if you can fix this mess I am responsible for, and fix my marriage, I will follow you and become a Christian. I will do whatever you tell me to do and call you my Lord. I am so very sorry for the things I have done and said! I have sinned against you so many times I don't know how you can ever forgive me now. But I believe my friend Phil Keaggy really does know you. And he said if I would just ask you, and admit that I am sinner lost in my sins, you would somehow forgive me. And when I die you will let me come be with you in heaven, so I don't have to burn for all eternity in hell. Oh God, I don't want to go to hell. I want to be with you forever!

As I was praying, I really felt like the Lord Jesus Christ of Nazareth himself was sitting in the empty seat next to me—just holding me. I could actually feel his arms round me as my eyes filled up with tears. I was immersed in his holy love.

It was like my Heavenly Father was saying, "I have been waiting so long for this moment. You came to the right place, my prodigal child. You can trust me with your life!" I could hear one of Phil's songs playing in my head, "All the Angels in Heaven Sing when there's a Soul Saved." [1]

---

1. From the album, "What A Day" (1973 released on New Song Records – now out of print)

Becoming Somebody New

When the plane landed I was a changed person. Something was very different. I knew that all my sins were forgiven—I could feel it deep inside! I was a new man, a new creation. I actually remember telephoning David from the airport to tell him I had arrived safely and was feeling much better than when I'd left. We had been friends for years at this point. When he heard my voice he asked, "Who is this speaking?"

I asked, "What do you mean? It's me!"

He replied, "Caspar? Well, you sound different somehow."

I was different somehow. One of my brothers–in–law, always very kind to me, came and picked me up from the airport. He wanted to get some coffee and counsel me. But I was on a mission now; I just had to see Joan first. When our eyes finally met and we embraced, I realized that the Lord fixed something that I could not have done. I still had a lot of work to do, but this time I was determined to get it right—to be there for my wife, to lay down my life for her.

There had been so many issues needing repair, but the Lord in His grace and mercy had already done that. What I needed to do now was simply appropriate it. Life is a process and a journey. There are always things to work on and improve in your walk with the Lord. You do it step by step.

If I were asked to walk from Liverpool to London it would seem overwhelming, but if I just started walking, taking one step at a time, eventually I would arrive there. It is much like this in many areas of one's life.

I knew I had baggage, but I was determined to walk in obedience to my Lord Christ Jesus. Now, mind you, there were places I was still not sanctified, but I did not have the understanding as yet to know how to repent of those things. Aren't you glad that the Lord is willing to take you and save you just the way He finds you—that you can come to Him just as you are?

We are all works in progress, and God is faithful and true and He will work out the details. It says in the Bible that as you make plans, the Lord directs your steps.

So enthusiastic was I about my newfound life that I was willing to give up art and music, but Joan always encouraged me to continue in my calling. Ever the adventurer, I wanted to try living in Australia, since I had some contacts there. But in the end we moved back to merry olde England. I had big plans to continue painting like the Pre–Raphaelites I so admired; the English countryside had so many places and scenes I wanted to turn into a work of art on canvas. But there was always the music. And before long I had formed a new band in Manchester.

It seemed for a time as though things were really looking up. We started playing in nearby Liverpool at some of the same places the Beatles once played before me. There was another band at that time from Ireland that I liked. And it seemed as though we were always playing at the same venue the week before or after they played there. They were called U2.

Soon I was immersed in my old ways again, staying up till all hours of the night practicing or playing concerts. One night we got home at 4 a.m., and left an hour later for a 7 a.m. live concert on the BBC. Who would even think to schedule a rock band at 7 a.m. anyway? But I was so driven to make a name for myself I would never question any scheduling issues.

A wonderful opportunity in Australia arose soon after this to open for the band 10CC, arranged by their drummer, my friend Paul Burgess. Paul had helped me a number of times and even played on my demo recordings. At that time, 10CC was huge and had big hit records, so I was now confident we'd get some real exposure.

We were all busy preparing to leave for Australia when we received the devastating news that 10CC's lead singer, Eric Steward, was in a terrible accident on the M1, England's major motorway. We were all very upset for Eric, and did not realize at first how badly he was injured. But it soon became apparent that 10CC's days were over. Our big world tour had ended before it had even begun. Some years later, I talked to Eric in London and was delighted to learn he was working with Paul McCartney on a recording. Eric had a hard time talking with me: I could still hear the effects of that accident in his voice.

But as this opportunity faded, other avenues started opening up. The music of the band The Police, with its occasional reggae sound (remember the song "Roxanne?") was gaining popularity and I had started playing with some of the famous Jamaican players in the reggae movement. I even had an offer to tour Germany with them. But the broken heart from my childhood combined with all my many recent disappointments (not to mention the misuse of my body) had begun to take their toll on me. My immune system had become seriously compromised and I came down with pneumonia. Instead of touring

Germany, I was laid up for a month, and by the time I recovered my band had fallen apart. It was back to Square One for the umpteenth time.

Sony Records & the Real John Lennon

As always seemed to happen, as soon as one door closed, another opened. This time was no different, but again it ended in tragedy. I was offered a deal with Sony Records. It came about because at the same time that John Lennon and Yoko Ono were recording in New York City, their producer, Jack Douglas, wanted to produce me as well. I was even invited to meet the Lennons. I figured I was certain to be asked to sing and play on their record. Even Tony Levin, Peter Gabriel's bass player, was on the project. I recall going to the Lennons' recording studio, the Hit Factory, and finding that the Lennons had just gone home for the day.

The studio was amazing. Yoko had brought in some of their living room furniture so they could feel more at home as they recorded their new album. They had long tables with all sorts of exotic foods and teas—just in case they had a desire for something. Yes, this must be the abundant life I had always heard about! Some of the engineers were still there and invited me back the next day.

But that was to become the fateful day that John Lennon was shot. Later that night my telephone would not stop ringing. People from around the world who knew I once played John Lennon on Broadway were calling. I guess they thought that if I answered the phone, maybe it was not true that Lennon had been fatally shot.

The whole world was buzzing with the news. I talked with someone who knew the policeman who put the wounded Lennon in a taxi to rush him to a nearby hospital. He told me the officer was asking Lennon questions and he was just moaning in pain. I always wondered: is it possible that in those last few minutes of his life John Lennon may have repented and cried out to God for His mercy and for the forgiveness of his sins? I hope so.

Of course, life continued, but everyone I knew was shaken to the core by John's untimely and shocking death. Sometime later I did a showcase (a sort of dress rehearsal for studio executives) for a fellow who was in the A & R department of Atlantic Records. Roger was a fellow Englishman who took a liking to my music and I had hopes he could help move my career along.

I was pressed into hiring a management team, who wasted no time in hiring Sid Bernstein, the fellow who is credited with bringing the Beatles to the States. His job was to get my team a meeting with the CEO of Atlantic Records. I had unknowingly done the groundwork and already had the support of the entire A&R department. So when the CEO asked his A&R department for feedback after listening to my demo, they all agreed it was a good move to sign me.

There used to be a joke in the record companies that went like this: How many A&R guys does it take to sign a new act? Answer: I don't know, how many do you think? It was the same joke about record company presidents. Basically, it meant that getting a record deal with a major label was almost impossible, because no one wanted to take responsibility; if the record flopped, the company would lose several hundred thousand dollars.

Of course, it could go the other way, as well. I watched some wonderful artists get turned down, and later, after they scored a hit, the same executives that turned them down would take complete credit among their peers, saying, "I discovered him!" Of course, no one dared ask, "Then why didn't you sign him?"

In my case, though, I knew I was on my way to being signed and doing a showcase performance was just a formality. The night I was to do the showcase for the CEO of Atlantic, I managed to hurt my fingers on my left hand moving my Marshal amp back a few feet. Unbeknownst to me, one of the technicians had removed a cover on the side to fix something and did not put the cover back. So my hand hit the little fan that is built into the amp to cool all the tubes. My fingers felt like someone ran over them. As if that wasn't enough, I then blew my voice out from over rehearsing and could not hit any of the high notes.

My back–up band had members from the Rolling Stones, Hall and Oats, and Santana. I gave it the best I could under the circumstances. Fortunately, I had a strong cheering section, including Joan and our dear friend Wes Pritchet, my friend Gene Neal and several others. Wes was a bass player who had started a band in the early 70's that became known as the Eagles. He later married and left the music world to become a success on Wall Street.

Star for a Season

When I got the record deal with Atlantic, I was already a born–again believer. Unfortunately, because I was just a baby believer, I did not know much of what the Bible said. Even worse, I also was not aware that I did not know very much!

Ahmed Ertegun, the CEO of Atlantic Records, had said at my audition that I was a virtuoso guitarist, with the moves and charisma of Mick Jagger as well as a strong singing voice. He was quoted later as having said at my audition that I would be the next Jimi Hendrix.

Atlantic Records started grooming me straightway to be the next "big thing."

If you recall, I had a blown voice and sore fingers during the showcase performance, but I was so driven and determined to be a rock star that I wasn't going to let anything get in my way. Little did I understand, though, that "we wrestle not against flesh and blood, but against principalities, against powers, against the rulers of this dark world, against spiritual wickedness in high places" (Ephesians 6:12). I didn't know it, but there were all sorts of invisible evil beings out there waiting to have their way with me. The Bible says that the devil comes for no other purpose than to kill, steal and destroy. One thing I have learned from all this is that most Christians do not really read their Bible; they really don't know what it says. And neither did I until recently.

My people are destroyed for lack of knowledge: Because thou hast rejected knowledge, I will also reject thee, that thou shalt be no priest to me: seeing thou hast forgotten the law of thy God, I will forget thy children. (Hosea 4:6)

As you read earlier, I did not grow up in the church. My father had once told me there was no such thing as an afterlife. He maintained that when you die you simply cease to exist. I've since learned that the sins of the father are passed on to the next generations. The things my father and his father struggled with are the things I had to deal with. The Bible calls it a curse. Thank God there is a way to break the curse because of what the Lord Jesus Christ did for us on the cross! I have since done as directed in II Chronicles 29 and confessed and acknowledged the sins of my fathers so that I and my children are now free from the penalty of their transgressions.

As a new Christian, I was trying hard to find the place where I might fit in. I kept asking myself what I was supposed to be doing in this secular music world as a follower of Jesus Christ. I reasoned that since most Christians don't buy all their goods from Christian vendors only, I should therefore have the freedom to express my music as it seemed right to me. I honestly thought my Christian beliefs and my music would come together in harmony, and that somehow I would find a way to make it work.

I didn't know that the change in my heart, now reflected in my music, would cause so many problems. No longer was I writing lyrics about the meaninglessness of life or the heartbreaks of love; now my music had a definite spirit of hope. I soon came up against a brick wall as I realized that the folks in the music business had other ideas. Record company executives started telling me what to wear, what to say and even what to write in my songs.

Atlantic Records' chairman of the board called me in one day to set things straight. I walked into the conference room and there he was sitting at this very long posh looking table. That position made him appear very powerful, bigger than life, while making me feel very small and inferior. "Is this a song about God?" he asked me accusingly. "If so, it's not getting on the album." It was, and it didn't.

And there were other conflicts. This was in the 1980s when Michael Jackson was on his way to super stardom. My producers were trying to push me into that dancing routine, if you can imagine that! They kept pushing me further and further from the rock and roll with which I was so comfortable and which came so naturally to me. I even submitted to being hypnotized once because my new producer wanted me to sound more like a black singer! I went through all sorts of emotional trials and tribulations back then, opening myself up more and more to an invisible world about which I knew nothing.

Then there was the life on the road that every recording artist has to endure. It wasn't what I'd imagined. We traveled continuously and the schedule allowed no regular times for meals and sleep. I even got to the point where I considered that this rock star stuff might not be worth it. I had just flown across the country, spending an entire day doing interviews with no time to rest or sit down to a proper meal. On trips like those, I barely got used to the time changes before we would be gone again. All for 45 minutes of glory in the spotlight! This life was not exactly rewarding.

Once I was in Seattle giving a concert, because one of my records had gotten a lot of radio play out there. We began by playing one song after another, none of which the audience had ever heard before. It was going over as well as could be expected, but when we began the song that was on the radio, the place just went wild. People started cheering once they finally made the connection. It has always seemed odd to me that people want to hear something they have already heard before, whereas I always seem to want to hear something new! It reminds me of my children when they were about three years old and would want me to read the same storybook to them every night.

Bon Jovi, Pat Benatar, Frampton & Sting

About the time I got my record deal with Atlantic, I was playing with the fabulous drummer Tico Torres and a talented fellow named Benji King on keyboards. Tico and Benji had met another fellow, a singer, whom they kept inviting me to come and meet. Instead of following that lead, I got involved doing recordings with Jan Hammer. Jan wrote the soundtrack for the television show "Miami Vice" which, although wonderful, in my opinion is not his best work, even though it is perhaps his most recognizable.

Tico and Benji ended up forming a new band with the singer they had met, who was none other than Bon Jovi! And the name of the new band? Bon Jovi, of course! Ironically, the recordings I made with Jan Hammer were never released.

Another story—yet another one that got away—involves a girl from Long Island who could really sing. A guitarist I had met while doing "Beatlemania" kept asking me to come out to Long Island and jam with him and this female vocalist. But when you live in New York City, there is an unwritten rule that you don't leave the City, but instead you wait for people to come to Manhattan. So I never did leave the City to jam with these musicians. As it turned out, the two got married and formed a band. The female vocalist was Pat Benatar.

Being stuck there, I never really enjoyed living in the city and, as soon as I got signed, we moved to upstate New York. There I would drive round at night and visit the local pubs with some mates of mine: Stanley Sheldon from the Peter Frampton band, and Lou Graham from Foreigner. Lou had a fantastic voice but was actually a bit on the shy side, I thought. Fans would often recognize Lou and ask for autographs and he would say, "Sorry, I am off duty now. Come see me when I am performing." One of the price tags of fame is not being able to move about freely. Often girls would assume, since I was with them, I must be Somebody, so they would ask me for autographs instead.

Speaking of Somebodies, I was backstage one time at one of those trendy clubs with some celebrity friends and a fellow came up to me and introduced himself as "Sting." I recall thinking, "Hmm. That is an odd sort of name." Then I had the thought, "Well, Caspar is sort of an odd name, as well." All the while the expression on this fellow's face was saying, "I cannot believe you don't know who I am!"

It may seem farfetched to be friends or acquaintances with some of these celebrities. But you must understand that in my business it was an everyday occurrence to associate with them. These were the days when I would be recording in the "A" room and Madonna would be in the "B" room next to me, and we'd trade recording stories.

There were days when I was really upset with my producers. One time, we were working on a recording and they were making comments like, "Okay, Caspar, that guitar is just great, but we're here to make something commercial that will sell. So give us 10% of what you just did. Keep it simple."

I felt like exerting my authority with, "Wait a minute fellows, I am the star here. I wrote the songs; I am the only one who knows how they are supposed to go!" But it really didn't matter what I said or how I played. They would just edit my work when I wasn't there. I wanted to go home and cry, "Look how they messed up my song, mum!"

But instead of saying anything to them that I would regret later, I just went out into the artist lobby area at Atlantic Records and practiced my guitar. I did not realize that. Harry Belafonte was sitting there listening to me. Before I even knew what happened, I was playing on the sound track of his movie, "Beat Street," with his express permission to play any way I wanted. His interest in me made quite an impact on my producers. The day after I recorded with Mr. Belafonte, their comments changed to, "Okay, Caspar, play any way you feel inspired!"

Mr. Belafonte was very good to me. After recording late one night, I missed my train, so he sent me home in his private limousine. I later showed him some of my artwork, and he looked at me and said, "These are great! If you ever need to fall back on another career you already have one." I had no idea what he was talking about. I was a rock star in the making! My future was assured! Little did I know just how prophetic those words were.

45

Being a painter, I often thought how wonderful it would be to draw and paint all the different places where I performed. But there was little time for my artwork then. Always on the road, I seemed to spend half my time in airports and the other half backstage. I found I wasn't alone in my disdain for this lifestyle: I remember seeing the graffiti that other band members who had been in a venue before me had scribbled on the walls—some very nasty things I would not ever share now. It always seemed odd to me that concert halls were all very nice and posh and yet backstage they looked pretty sleazy. Things were not as they seemed.

On the road, nothing was what you might consider "normal." My band and I ate very late at night because there were so many radio and television interviews. We slept little and it seemed as though we traveled nonstop at times. At one point, my drummer and I had a conversation after a flight to the West Coast. He asked, "Did you sleep last night?"

"No." I answered, "Did you?"

Shaking his head, he asked, "How long has it been this time?"

"Three days!"

We both suffered from insomnia and were about to play a television concert in a few minutes. It was like being on an adrenaline high for days on end and we just had no other choice but to go on. Today, I know what's behind insomnia. It's a form of fear that comes from taking thought for tomorrow—also known as worry—which the Lord said not to do!

I couldn't change my days on the road, but I did help change some of the behavior of the people who were on the road with me. Guys in the band and crew would hide stuff when I came down the hallway or entered a room. They'd whisper, "Caspar's coming!" and stuff pornography under the bed or shove the groupie girls into the closet. I sometimes knew what was going on but decided it was not up to me to judge anyone, as that job belongs to the Lord. I think just showing up and not saying anything was pretty convicting.

The rock and roll thing is an evil trap to many people, young and old. Anyone hanging around in those circles is liable to be sucked down into the pit—even though there is some good stuff mixed in with it. The analogy I have for it now is getting a very posh, exquisite dinner laced with just a touch of poison. Our enemy the devil works like that. He will quote Holy Scripture out of context so it appears good, sounds good, but is so wrong! Just look at how he misquoted Scripture to Jesus when he tempted him! No wonder he is called the great deceiver.

The Guy with the Tongue

Another thing I experienced frequently as an up–and–coming rock musician was being suddenly befriended by a lot of very famous rock stars, people like Gene Simmons and Paul Stanley of Kiss. I recall once when Gene telephoned me and my wife answered. I was sound asleep, after just getting back from somewhere, and she was pushing the telephone in my face saying, "Some friend of yours named Gene Simmons wants to talk with you... Say, wait a minute, is that the guy with the TONGUE?" I knew he heard her comments, and fortunately, he laughed. He was also the fellow who talked me into getting my first answering machine, confronting me with the fact that he had tried reaching me for a few weeks to no avail. He simply asked, "What kind of artist can afford to miss that one important call?" I went out that very day and got one.

We had long, deep conversations and to this day I still feel a great love for Gene and Paul. We'd talk about Old Testament scriptures;

Gene really knew a lot about Jewish customs. In fact, a number of my celebrated friends seemed genuinely interested in finding some sort of spiritual truth, yet their lives were full of superficiality and devoid of anything of value. A rock star might ride around in a limousine all day, as I once did, but he is still just another guy in the end. He might have more fame than he could enjoy, and more money than a person could ever spend, yet he's still empty inside unless he asks the Lord to fill that emptiness. There is an empty space in every heart that can only be filled with the love, grace and mercy of the Lord Jesus Christ. Anything else we try and put in there will eventually leak out. I speak from personal experience.

Back in those days of concert tours, my reviews were certainly very favorable, but often it wasn't enough. Sometimes I would unknowingly snub someone from the press, just because there wasn't enough of me to give everyone an interview and offer them my undivided attention. This resulted more than once in unkind articles being written about me. I recall one instance when, at a press conference just prior to a concert, I chose to give an interview to the big newspaper and I basically had to ignore the reporter from a little college paper. The major newspaper gave me a very positive review, while the college paper blasted me out of the water.

I was very ill at the time with a fever and a bad cold. But as the saying goes, "the show must go on." After three songs, it dawned on me that I had just given all I had to give, but the contract said we still had another 40 minutes on stage! Somehow I just carried on, relying on my guitar expertise to cover my weakened vocals. I was a professional, and was not about to let the audience know I was sick. I continued to the end by pacing myself as a runner does in the last stages of a cross—country race. It takes a lot of physical stamina, strength and power to sing a concert—let alone play an instrument at the same time.

Gene Simmons happened to be playing a concert there the following week, and telephoned to read me the bad review from the college paper. He gave me good advice: ignore the write–up and carry on as if it never happened. Any publicity is good as long as people hear about you. He reminded me of some of the nasty things people said about him and his band in papers and magazines. Gene was always encouraging and acted somewhat parental towards me.

In the end, his good words were forgotten. I got a telephone call from my manager's office. They had just gotten hold of that particular article, and proceeded to reprimand me for days. It was just one person's comments and opinions but it became a thunderstorm in my life. My management team knew how sensitive and vulnerable I could be, and seemed to know how to manipulate and control me to the point of tears. In the Bible, manipulation is also called witchcraft. It certainly had power over me!

I could dwell on one negative comment to the point where a spirit of depression would overtake me and sometimes I would even consider ending my life. How many times must I have invited the spirit of death to come and destroy me? How many times did I let the enemy use my own voice against me? How many times do you think you have let the enemy speak through you?

I have attended a number of churches where they teach that once the Holy Spirit lives inside you, evil spirits cannot have any effect on you. Now, I would simply ask them why so many Christians are troubled and tormented. Why do Christians act just like the unsaved so much of the time? Most Christians are certainly not manifesting the Holy Spirit all the time, are they? Could it be that they have not cleansed their spirits of evil according to 2nd Corinthians 7:1?

Having therefore these promises, dearly beloved, let us cleanse ourselves from all filthiness of the flesh and spirit, perfecting holiness in the fear of God.

Is this to say your spirit can get dirty? Let's see what Paul said in Romans 7:17:

Now then it is no more I that do it, but the sin that dwelleth in me.

May I be so bold as to suggest that an evil spirit can "have" a believer? That is, have at least partial control of them.

At least now I am no longer ignorant. Somewhere along the way, you or I may have given the enemy what I call a door point into our lives. Although we have given every inch of ourselves to the Lord, the enemy was still able to get back in. How? We give him a place through our sin. Say, for example, we hold unforgiveness towards ourselves or others, or even towards God. The Bible tells us that if we don't forgive others—or ourselves—God will not forgive us. Matthew 6:14–15 says,

For if ye forgive men their trespasses, your heavenly Father will also forgive you:
But if ye forgive not men their trespasses, neither will your Father forgive your trespasses.

Have you ever said you've forgiven someone but deep down you are still holding a grudge? When you think of or see that person do you get a high–octane "ping" in the pit of your stomach? This is usually a pretty good indication that you really haven't forgiven them. Do you know that frequently the one we have the most difficult time forgiving and accepting is ourselves? Either we flat out disagree with the way God made us, or we live with guilt and shame because of things we have done in the past. I will tell you the truth: forgive yourself and others whether you feel like it or not. No one can afford not to do what God has commanded us to do! So *DO IT NOW* in the name of our Lord Jesus Christ of Nazareth!

Solo Success

My life as a recording artist for Atlantic Records had a lot of ups and downs, but in retrospect it was mostly down. I felt like I had lost control of my life and given it over to my managers. They had power of attorney and made many decisions that were not in my best interests. I had become a slave to a life that was no longer mine! I felt abandoned most of the time and could not understand why everything seemed so difficult.

Even with the band, there was always this invisible line that we could never cross. I was the star, which made me the boss. So when I played them a new song I had just written, I never knew if they really liked it or if they just said they did so as not to make waves. They were like hired guns to help me in my quest for hit records.

One of the songs from my solo album made its way up in the trade charts like Billboard and Cash Box after the record company did a re—mix to promote it to the dance clubs. This resulted in offers to play some clubs in New York City for a hefty amount of money. I was thrilled, until I discovered they were mostly gay clubs. The AIDS epidemic had just become a real concern and no one was certain yet exactly how it was transmitted. I told my manager I would not play in those places. Instead, we were booked in everything from motorcycle hard rock clubs to trendy pop clubs.

My friend Kenny Fischer hand–built a couple of special guitar amplifiers for me about this time, which he let me help design from a suggestion I made. They became known as Train Wreck Amps. The first one was called "Ginger," which was Joan's nickname. Everyone who heard it at Atlantic Records wanted one. I just loved it; that amp produced what became my signature sound for years to come. You'll find it written up in *Who's Who in Amplification* (Webber). Right about then, things started to look promising again. People in the industry were taking notice of my playing and unique sound. Rumor in the industry had it yet again that I might be the next "big thing."

I went to see Phil Keaggy play one night after I finished a showwhen we were both in the same town. His was like a classical concert, with people quietly listening, and I found myself being envious. The group I had just finished playing to was a rough bunch. Smoke bombs went off during our set. Girls threw their unmentionables on stage. People were drunk or high on drugs. And fist–fights were always breaking out. Record company guys would tell me how cool I was to come out and stare down the audience. Little did they know that with all the spotlights in my face, I couldn't even see the audience! They mistook my squints for machismo. After seeing Phil's gig, I became somewhat jealous—I wanted what he had.

Later that night, I sat in Phil's car playing song ideas for him—songs with titles such as, "I Learned to Turn to Jesus." My record company was not interested in these songs. If I couldn't do them, maybe some-one else would. I told Phil I wanted to walk out of my record deal, leave secular rock and roll, and follow after the Lord. He just said, "My brother, it is really hard to do what I am doing." It seemed to me that what he was doing couldn't be harder than what I was doing. Once again he was right. It was very much harder.

A Time to be Born and a Time to Die

In 1984 Joan and I were expecting our first child, but I was gone during most of her pregnancy, finding myself either crisscrossing the country or stuck in a recording studio. One weekend, we were working on my first album and the producers kept me working for two days straight with no rest! They only allowed me to go when I told them my wife was due at any moment. I recall them asking if I could be back in four or five hours. I got home and collapsed. As soon as I lay down, Joan told me it was time to take her to the hospital. Unable to rouse myself, I kept nodding off and she would yell, "How can you sleep at a time like this?" We finally did get to the hospital where poor Joan labored for 23 hours. It was a difficult birth, and I don't know if I was much help, but finally she gave birth and we were delighted to meet Derek, our first child. At least I was there!

By this time, I had been awake for over three days, and after Derek's birth, went home to get some sleep. A friend of ours named Angela was staying over to help Joan. I made one telephone call to a friend in London to tell him about Derek and then the thought came to me that perhaps I should try and contact my father to tell him about his grandson. We had not spoken in years, but I did have his telephone number which was written on a letter he had written to me years before

He had come to see me play a concert but did not even try and go backstage. Instead, he wrote me a letter. In the letter he told me he was amazed that I actually had my name up in lights on the big marquee and that I seemed to have a number of fans. But there the compliments ended, and he continued with criticism of my performance. At one point I had turned my back on the audience to adjust something on the amplifier. This, he said, was very unprofessional and he told me so in no uncertain terms.

My father's telephone number was on that letter, but I was much too tired to attempt to reconcile with him right then. So I went to bed and had just fallen asleep when Angela came and woke me up. She told me I had an urgent phone call. I learned that my father had been murdered.

My sister's abusive husband had been beating her, and since Joan had known first hand how that might end up, we sent my sister some money so she could take her child and go someplace safe. I had warned her not to return to our father, knowing that was the first place her husband would look for her. But she moved back in with him anyway. Her estranged husband then came over and shot our father in the back, my sister and her two–year–old son watching in horror.

In spite of this devastating news, I could not leave my family to help my sister. I went back to the hospital, trying my best not to let Joan know what had happened. After just a few minutes she saw through my feeble efforts. Out of all the rock and roll friends I had, there was no one we could turn to for help. My managers and press agent told me not to tell anyone because of the bad publicity it would create. The only person I told was my friend Steve Hayes, who fixed my guitars. The Church of England we attended when I was in town sent over the priest. He did some ritual called "last rites," which made no sense to me. I did know one thing, though. I knew instinctively I had to get down on my knees to ask the Lord to forgive this man who killed my father. Then I forgave him myself.

Words that Wound

My father was living in the States when he was killed, and I was in New York, unable to attend the funeral. One of my relatives, out of exasperation, grief or whatever, telephoned me and told me she felt I was to blame for my father's death. . She reasoned that if I had not interfered, my sister and her husband would have worked out their domestic differences and my father would still be alive.

Today, I would know how to reject those words—not taking them into my spirit. But back then, ignorant and unlearned in Scripture, I thought her accusation was deserved. I believed that it was my fault. My earthly father always told me I was not good at handling life's complex situations, and here was proof.

The following day, I was forced to go back into the recording studio. I kept trying to hide my pain, but it started showing through. My producers could not understand why asking me to make an adjustment in my performance could now reduce me to tears. My managers tried to cover for me, but I was falling apart. The interviews I did must have seemed like I was on something—which in my business was quite normal. I grew sadder by the day. I lost my focus, and the songs I was required to write every month for my publisher became more and more cryptic.

Six months later, I was driving home from the studio and trying to find something good to listen to on the radio. A folk song came on. I was about to switch stations, except that the vocalist was singing about a father who never had time for his son, and when the son grew up he did not have time for the father. The song was, "Cats in the Cradle," by Harry Chapin, and the message really bothered me.

I got home and the telephone rang. While I picked it up, my little son Derek was smiling at me, saying, "Da–da." The voice on the phone told me I was leaving in one week to tour Japan and then Australia. I looked at Derek and out of my mouth came the words, "No, I am not going!" The voice on the other end of the phone was screaming at me. I put down the phone and picked up my son, and thus ended my career with Atlantic Records. I was kept on a retainer for almost a year as my manager kept hoping I would come back to my senses.

One day the telephone rang and I was told if I did not start performing again I would be sued. I hung up and watched Derek, then about two years old, falling asleep. I prayed, "Oh God, I am not ready to go back out. Please help me. I can't leave our son; he needs me here." A short time later the telephone rang again and this time, I was told not to worry. If I would just keep writing songs they were willing to wait until I was ready to perform again. I was just in awe how the Lord answered my prayer. The invisible God in Heaven had just reached down and orchestrated peace in my life and career.

Taking Thoughts Captive

I wanted to serve the Lord but my biggest obstacle was my financial dependence on writing songs for a secular audience. There were many conflicts, as you may well imagine. And without much Bible knowledge, I was perishing. A very dark force was orchestrating a plan to destroy me just as it does all believers, because Satan is real, and he has unchanging goals: to steal, kill and destroy.

If you find that the words and thoughts in your head do not line up with the word of God, then please take this advice: Don't listen to lies! Let's face it; the real battle for your life begins in your mind. You can't do anything without thinking thoughts about it first, and that's why the Lord tells us to take our thoughts captive. If you don't, they will take you captive! We need to be good soldiers and understand the enemy's tactics and know how to defend ourselves!

> *For though we walk in the flesh, we do not war after the flesh: For the weapons of our warfare are not carnal, but mighty through God to the pulling down of strong holds: Casting down imaginations, and every high thing that exalteth itself against the knowledge of God, and bringing into captivity every thought to the obedience of Christ.*
> *(II Corinthians 10:3–5)*

How many thoughts? Every thought! That means *every thought* must line up with the Word of God. Your enemy knows how to work you over through your thoughts and imaginations.

It is still important to me to play skillfully unto the Lord. *"Sing unto Him, a new song: play skillfully with a loud noise,"* Psalm 33:3. It's what I learned to do all those years in secular music. The Lord does not waste anything in his economy. Years later, I am still able to sing new songs—and I can still play with a loud noise! But now that I have learned how to take my thoughts captive, my music is much more meaningful and rewarding. I have a reason and a purpose now for my music.

I have repented to the Lord and now refuse to ever "perform" again. Instead, when I go out to play a concert, I am there simply to share my gifts in music. (I have also made the discovery that the world won't fall apart if I don't play at my optimum level every time.)

Release Us from Religion!

I can't find any question that the Bible does not address. The other day after a church service, an elderly woman started telling me that any music performed with an electric guitar is demonic. I have had my fair share of similar conversations over the years. I wanted to point out that I believed anyone wearing the color red, as she was, was demonic, but thank God I have learned to bridle my tongue!

Once, after playing the opening act for Phil Keaggy and Randy Stonehill, a youth pastor grabbed me as I walked off the stage. I had just receiving a standing ovation, but he angrily raked me over the coals, saying my music was of the devil, and did so in full view of a number of reporters from the press. My pastor, overhearing the commotion, interceded for me.

After everyone had left, the youth pastor came back to apologize. Even though I was really affected by his outburst, I knew I had to forgive him in Jesus' name. Sometimes your feelings are not even yours, so you need to forgive others whether you "feel" like it or not. Your very life may depend upon it, because I tell you again; if you do not forgive others, God says he will not forgive you.

> *For if ye forgive men their trespasses, your heavenly Father will also forgive you:*
> *But if ye forgive not men their trespasses, neither will your Father forgive your trespasses. (Matthew 6:14–15)*

I've had a number of religious individuals confront me over the years. I've learned to recognize when a legalistic and unclean religious spirit has a foothold inpeople. The Bible tells *believers* not to give any place to the devil, so that would mean that it is possible for a spirit-filled believer to have an unclean spirit. If the enemy has lost you to the Lord, he doesn't just give up and go away! He looks for a way to get in and frequently he uses spiritual pride to try and take you down. In a deceptive way, he will convince you that you know so much more than the other saints. And spiritual pride can sound so convincing!

How can I be so sure that my music was not of the devil? I really had to seek the Lord on this issue. I asked him to show me if anything I was playing was not pleasing to him—even to the point of giving up music altogether if that was his will. At times the opposition from others was so great that I did try and stop playing music for good. Then, out of nowhere, someone would stop me in a parking lot and say something like, "I saw you play a concert and you sang this song and I gave my life to Jesus that night." Then they would tell me how God has been blessing them and how they are now serving him.

I would be so convicted of my foolishness and think, "Oh, Lord how did I ever get to a place where I would not even want to use the gifts you gave me? Please forgive me Lord, and lead me on to the next place to minister." Which is more important—seeing someone receive salvation and be set free, or going along with religious tradition?

Caspar and the Newsboys, 1999

Caspar and Joan at awards ceremony, 1990

Pastor Henry Wright, 2004

McClouds Family, 1998

Caspar and author Robert Lacey, 2000

Caspar and Peter Fuler of the Newsboys 1999

Caspar and Gypsy, 1991

Phil Keaggy and Caspar in Concert 1990

Caspar and Gypsy, 1997

Caspar and Gypsy, 2002

Caspar recording for Atlantic Records, 1981

Randy Stonehill and Caspar, 1989

Joan and her twin Jean, 1980

Recording for Atlantic Records, 1982

Caspar at early Christian concert, 1987   Caspar in Manchester England, 1970's

Recording for Atlantic Records, 1982

Joan McCloud, 1970's

Conway Castle in Wales, 1980's

Caspar captures Joan, 1977

My horse "Mr. Bob" poses for portrait, 2004

Caspar and THREE in Concert, 2004

Press clippings of my early life in showbiz

Atlantic Record Tour, 1984

From left to right: Mark Alexander,

Dave Beal (on drums), Caspar,

Matt Bassionett, and Greg Houstead

Music in the Master's Hands

One night at a concert I found myself unwilling to play a song I had written about a friend who had died suddenly from a brain aneurism. The words told how I had always meant to share the gospel with her, but it never quite seemed like the right time and finally it was too late. My friend was deeply into the New Age movement and because I was such a recent believer, I did not have the knowledge to explain the truth to her. She sent me letters about her forays into the occult, which included séances, trances and spirit guides. The enemy has always used the same lie ever since the Garden of Eden to tempt people to dabble with the occult: "*Surely ye will not die.*" This "New Age" philosophy is really just a bunch of repackaged, age–old lies.

Anyway, I would read her letters and not know what to do. Being a new believer, I did not know that during a seance an evil spirit could use someone's body or voice. Disembodied spirits have no means of expression unless they convince people to allow them to operate through them. My friend was a very nice and kind person—like so many other wonderful, decent people walking about this planet. She was just being used by the enemy and was not even aware of it.

You can sometimes lead a New Ager along the path to salvation and sanctification more easily than others who are not much interested in the things of the spirit. You just have to help them test all spirits against the Holy Word of God to see whether they are true or a lie.

It always makes me feel sad when I think about people who are lost forever. How the Lord must grieve over them!

Sometimes when I played the song I mentioned earlier, I actually got teary–eyed and so I came to the point where I just did not want to play it anymore. But that particular night, my friend Joe Harrison was with me and he kept asking me to play it. So I relented and played the song. Later I learned that a teenage girl was planning on committing suicide that very night after the concert and instead gave her life to the Lord.

At that same concert, a young man came forward and asked to speak with one of the ministers. He explained that he was a drug dealer with more than fifty thousand dollars in cash in his pockets from recent deals. He gave his life to the Lord during that song and wondered what he should do with the money now that he was a Christian.

The Lord used that song again that night in a tremendous way. It was a concert with another full house and from on stage, all I could see was a sea of teenagers. The Holy Spirit knew what I was supposed to do and say. So before I played a note, I prayed that the Lord would use me as his instrument—that the people would experience him and not me. Finishing the song, I invited the teens to raise their hands if they wanted to receive forgiveness and salvation from God. So many hands were raised that there were not enough ministers to do follow–up. Unbeknownst to me, the night before a young girl from a youth group in that community had died from an aneurism, just like the girl in my song.

These are just a few examples of the incidents that helped persuade me to keep doing what I felt all along the Lord was calling me to do—in spite of all those in the church who criticize non–traditional music. God gave us all different fingerprints, so just maybe he likes a variety in music, too!

I once wrote an instrumental called, "A Night in the Holy Land." I love to explain how this piece came about. I had a dream that I was back in time 2,000 years ago. In the dream, I clearly heard very unusual music that was obviously indigenous to that ancient time period, but the sounds were made by an electric guitar. Were any of us there 2,000 years ago? How do we know no such music existed then? Music is only a vehicle to get you from one place into another. It changes with time just the way the style of clothing changes, just the way automobile chassis change. It's the spirit behind the music that's important.

I think music can and is being used of the enemy, but so is it used of God. To say that a particular beat or style is demonic seems to me to be a futile argument. Did you know that some of the sacred music found in today's hymnals is actually old English and German drinking songs re–fitted with Christian lyrics? An example of this is "A Mighty Fortress Is Our God," a tune which was sung in pubs long before it was sung in church.

Martin Luther was not only a great reformer, he was a musician as well. Although most people seem to think of him as a theologian, turned Bible translator, who became a fiery preacher and political leader. As a musician he was bent on restoring worship back into the church. He apparently used some of the popular secular songs of his day that were often sung in public drinking houses, otherwise known as taverns. Perhaps he thought to himself, "Why should the devil have all the good music?"

This was actually a common practice of borrowing a popular song and changing its lyrics. Just consider for a moment if you will, a song sung in England that I learned known as "God Save the Queen." In the United States it is same song sung with different words known as " My Country 'Tis of Thee." An excellent book to read on this subject is "Don't Stop The Music," by Ed DeGarmo and Dana Key.

I agree with J. S. Bach: the only reason to make music is for the glory of God. And instead of defending rock and roll, I will only say that if God can make a donkey speak (Numbers 22), then he can use whatever he wants! He can even use you and me. And He uses rock and roll!

Don't Touch the Altar!

Here is one last humorous example of the foolishness of arguing against rock and roll. Representatives from a Catholic Church asked me to minister through a concert. This happened to be a church where the bishop resided, so they had to form a committee to interview me. I drove several hours at their request, and when I walked into the room, I noticed that they were all wearing dark suits and ties. I wasn't. It was West Palm Beach, Florida, and it was August.

The committee started in with a long list of questions. One of them said to me, "I can't find any problems with your lyrics, but your music sounds very much like the music we hear on the secular radio." I pushed my seat back from the table where we sat and looked at my accusers. "Gentlemen, I drove a long way to attend this meeting and I just want to ask you one question, How did you get here? Did you also drive a car?"

Like dry English humor, it took a moment to sink in, but suddenly they understood. Both Christians and non–Christians use the same type of cars to get where they need to go. Christian musicians can use secular music to get across a very non–secular, God–glorifying message to their listeners. Even more important, it might be the only type of music that many young people would be willing to listen to. The message must come through the music with which the audience is comfortable. Once this realization sunk in, the "suits" decided I was welcome to perform in their church.

When the big day arrived, Joe Harrison briefed me on what <u>not</u> to do in a Catholic Church. Somewhat apprehensive, I entered the building and headed down a hallway to the main sanctuary. Two nuns where ahead of me, not knowing I was behind them. I heard one remark to the other, "Oh, I hope and pray this Caspar fellow doesn't jump up on our altar like they do on MTV!"

I thought, "How does <u>she</u> know what they do on MTV?"

Joe's final instruction had been, "Whatever you do, <u>do not</u> touch the altar! During the concert one of the microphones went out, and our sound tech immediately laid out all his gear on the altar, using it as a workbench. Talk about amazing grace—no one took our sound tech out to stone him! What's more, after the concert they wanted to book us for the following year. Praise God, some good seeds were planted that night.

The Roots of Disease Bear Fruit

Unfortunately, all throughout my Atlantic Record days my health began to deteriorate. Allergies were a way of life for me; I always felt congested, and sleeping only made it worse. It seemed I was continually taking medicine for various problems just to get through another day.

After Atlantic, my career was not going the way I wanted, and I started searching for something I did not quite understand yet. Sometimes I would just break down and cry in the dressing rooms or at the recording studio. I found out that you can only internalize so much stuff before it finds a way out. Denying my problems, I pretended I was just fine. Stiff upper lip and all that sort of thing.

Looking back, I realize now that a broken heart was causing a lot of my problems.

When you haven't been loved the way God intended for you to be loved, the door opens in your heart for a spirit of fear to come in (I John 4:18). All allergies can be traced to a breakdown in the immune system, which results from a person being in fear. Entertaining feelings of dread and dwelling on anxious thoughts releases a hormone named cortisol into your blood system. Long—term, the continual release of cortisol begins to damage your body's immune system and opens you to all manner of sickness.[2] For every thought we have there is a conscious or unconscious reaction, a chemical hormone or nerve signal that is activated.

> *Casting down imaginations, and every high thing that exalts itself against the knowledge of God, and bringing into captivity every thought to the obedience of Christ. (II Corinthians 10:5—6)*

Satan and his kingdom can control you physiologically through thoughts and actions. If you don't believe me, study your Bible! Just be sure you have a King James Version and a *Strong's Concordance* so you can look up the original Greek and Hebrew meanings. (I believe that all the modern translations contain many mistakes and errors. If these translations contain so many errors, doesn't it stand to reason that they make it very difficult to know what God really said?)[3]

---

2. See Henry Wright (1999) *A More Excellent Way*, Pleasant Valley Publications, Thomaston, Georgia

3. See Appendix, Teaching on Translations

Goodbye Atlantic, Now What?

When I left Atlantic Records, I decided that I was not going to play music anymore unless it was to the glory of my God. The only problem was I did not have anything else lined up! I just wanted out. I was now married with a child and so I escaped back to England, living in London without a clue as to what I was supposed to do next. I thought

I was supposed to be a rock star but at this point, no one except a few in the music industry seemed to believe it.

Without Atlantic Records, I was losing my fan base. It was like starting all over again. I was so troubled inside that I think I did not even come out of our flat in London for over a month, avoiding everyone and everything. I tried to reconnect as a husband and father, but this did not come easily either. Part of me was saying, "Wait, I am a rock star." The other part was saying, "No, you're just a loser." I was an emotional mess. Whose voice was I listening to now? I was a believer but I was listening to the voice of depression.

Even though I had offers to play for other bands—and had record deals as a solo artist—I could not seem to get anything together. I felt ill most of the time, physically fighting a host of allergies and emotionally battling spirits of depression.

As a young Christian, new in my faith, I struggled spiritually as well. Joan and I started going to a very old church in London, but we knew no one who had genuine faith. Every Sunday, it seemed that the small congregation of 15 or so in this magnificent building—which could have held a thousand or more—was sitting with spider webs covering them from the week before. The words the Pastor spoke seemed empty and were devoid of any of the power so often spoken about in the Bible. Have you ever attended a church like that?

A Painting for the Prince

During this time of introspection and upheaval, we spent time with a friend named Helen who also became our nanny. She actually was the sister of my friend Lawrence who introduced me to Joan. Helen was dating a man from Buckingham Palace and he managed to bring my artwork to the attention of the Prince of Wales. Helen was one of my biggest encouragers. She must have thought if only Prince Charles and Princess Diana could see my work, surely I would become a court painter for the Royal Family! It was rather a nice thought that entertained us for a week or two.

Soon, I received a letter inviting me to bring a painting to Buckingham Palace. I remember showing my letter at the front gate and the guard, who had a very thick Cockney accent, said with a smile, "Right this way, gov'na." And off we went into the inner courts. I could not help but notice that at every point where I was asked to show my letter of passage, the officers' accents became more and more refined! Actually, they started sounding like Paddington Bear, who was a very popular cartoon character in England at that time.

When I finally entered the offices of the Prince of Wales, it seemed a bit like one of those James Bond movies with all the high–tech gear. You'd just wave your hand across a beam of light and these massive doors would open automatically. Approaching the desk in the Prince's office, I stated my business to an officer who was like a grouchy old ex–navy commander. He took my letter and rudely started firing questions at me. I stumbled over the name of the personal secretary to Prince Charles and he grew even more crusty, thinking to give me a hard time. "Hmm. So you come from the North, do you?" he said, as a snobby put–down. Then I was informed that he had no prior notice of my arrival. He would have to "make enquiries" about me.

When he left, my mind drifted off and I started imagining what it must have been like to incur the wrath of the King and end up in the Tower of London. Very horrible things in history have happened in the Tower. With my imagination running away with me, I felt trapped and found myself wishing I had never come.

The officer returned before I could flee, saying, "Please sit over there." I looked and there were many empty chairs. Which one did he mean? I felt like he must have meant the last one, furthest away from his desk. The atmosphere in the room was thick with tension. The class system is very strong in England. You're either one of the privileged, or one of "them." The few minutes I had to wait seemed like hours.

Suddenly, the telephone rang. I heard Officer Grumpy say repeatedly, "Yes, sir! Straightaway, sir!" And almost as if it were a new day, Officer Grumpy's rough demeanor disappeared and a very courteous manner took its place. Would I care for some champagne? Tea then? Perhaps some sherry? Did I fancy anything else? I remember wondering how he could change his personality so quickly, so dramatically. The Bible clearly tells us to treat everyone the same whether poor or wealthy.

I was soon ushered into the secretary's office and had the great honor of presenting my watercolor depicting a woman groom with a polo pony. The favorable response I received was very encouraging.

The very next day, while I was at home, Helen came and found me, explaining there were two special Palace guards at the door. Once again I started panicking, thinking someone must have pinched the Palace cutlery and they were going to try and blame me! Instead, the guards presented a letter signed by Prince Charles and Princess Diana expressing their deep gratitude at the gift of my painting. They used words like, "splendid," and "magnificent." At first, the unloving spirits I had grown up with filtered my reading and I thought they were making fun of me and my work. Reading the letter again, however, I realized they were conveying genuine appreciation. This was a defining moment and I began painting horses in earnest after that.

That was, until health problems repeatedly got in the way. Great opportunities came up, like having an exhibit at a world class horse show, but I would be too ill to attend. My physical health grew worse. Meanwhile, my poor wife missed her family in the States terribly, and since I was in ill health most of the time, the decision was made that we would move back to New York.

A church in New York gave me my first official job in music ministry. My job was to write new songs and play a concert once a month. Every month, more and more people showed up and I was able to "rock the church out" at a time when it was not acceptable. My role model was Phil Keaggy—I just did what I had learned from him. I wrote music that I wanted to hear. The blessing and surprise came when people got saved at my concerts.

We weren't able to stay long, though, as my failing health prohibited regular work. To be nearer to Joan's sisters we moved to West Palm Beach, Florida. There I was given a church staff position as an "artist in residence," just like they did for my childhood hero Leonardo da Vinci! They paid a small salary and I did what I loved doing—sharing the Gospel, painting, and playing in all three morning services. We also sponsored a monthly concert series, in which Phil Keaggy and Randy Stonehill participated.

My friends Joe and Pat Harrison convinced me to start recording again. They helped me out in many ways, and paid for a large part of the new recording. I played more concerts and made my first Christian CD album, which got on the charts. Unfortunately, things still didn't come together. First, Christian radio seemed to be controlled by people in Nashville who viewed me as a secular artist. Then, I could not get my record distributed very well. Finally, the church I worked for split, and I became very disillusioned. As the disappointments mounted, my health declined. I could not help but wonder why my life was such a mess.

Yet Another Move

For many years, my friends in the music industry kept encouraging me to move closer to Nashville, Tennessee. By this time, I had so many close friends in Florida that it took a long while before we were convinced to leave. One such friend was Gene Klein, who had become like a grandfather to Derek—and a father to me. Gene was a retired engineer and had an IQ close to genius level. He taught me many practical things I should have known but never learned. Gene could do just about anything and he was always willing to give me wise counsel.

Other people also made the decision to leave Florida very difficult. My friends Jerry and Joy Thomas were like a brother and sister to me. They let me ride and care for their horse, Gypsy, as if he were mine. I learned more about riding from hands—on work with him than in all the riding classes I ever took. Gypsy did not have brakes back then, so I never knew if he would stop when I wanted him to. But by the time I had to move away, he would do just about anything for me.

Robert Lacey, however, was a very strong voice urging me not to give up and to follow my dreams. We met because our young sons were in Christian school together. Robert and his family lived at the very posh Palm Beach Polo Club. He was able to afford to send his son to this exclusive school. My son, on the other hand, was there because his daddy was on staff at the church! Robert was a best—selling author who later became the royal biographer for Queen Elizabeth II, and I highly valued his opinion. He came to one of my concerts one night and we ate together afterwards. "Don't give up, Caspar," he counseled. "Take this offer from that agency and move to Atlanta and see where your musical talent will take you."

That sealed it. The day we finished packing for Atlanta, I took Gypsy out for one last gallop. Then I had a late dinner with Jerry and Joy. As we were saying farewell, Jerry—who is really bright and a big, strong fellow—started to weep, saying he was losing his best friend. I never really saw that side of him before that day, or just had not connected with it. Then we all just lost it and wept.

When we arrived at the new house in Atlanta, my wife and children (by then the Lord had added Hayley, a daughter, to our family) started to cry. It was a very difficult time and we almost moved back to Florida the next day. But Gene gave me wise counsel to stay with the decision we had made.

On Stage with the Newsboys

After a few months in Atlanta, I met and became friends with the Newsboys, since we had the same booking agent. They were all very encouraging to me, and asked my new band, Three, to open their concert. There was some sort of mix–up, and after arriving with all our gear, the sound crew was not prepared for us to play that night. The opening band instead was Petra.

I had been sitting backstage with Matt McCoy and Kerry Severin. These guys are like real brothers to me and I was really looking forward to playing for them. I did not want to accept that it was not going to happen. But we all just began praying and encouraging each other in the Word– mostly that the Word would change the lives of those who came this night regardless of whether we played or not.

It was five minutes to show time, but only The Newsboys' drummer Duncan Phillips was there. The promoter was pacing back and forth muttering, "Where are they? They're on in five minutes—what are we going to do?" throwing his hands up in the air each time he said it.

Duncan was sipping a drink and looking very calm. "No worries, mate," he replied, "They'll be here on time."

Just then, the backstage door opened and in walked the rest of the Newsboys, approaching very casually like they had all the time in the world. Whilst the promoter was on his knees giving thanks to God that the band finally showed up, Peter Furler walked over to me, put his hand on my shoulder and said, "Look mate, I heard what happened tonight. Tell me, what Newsboy songs do you know?"

I knew straightway that he meant to find out which songs I knew so I could play and sing with them. And as for that, I did not really know any songs, as I mostly just do my own material. But my son, a huge Newsboys fan, had played their recordings so much that I was familiar with some. I looked back at Peter and said, "I sort of know that song called, 'Breakfast.'"

He replied, "Great! When we start that song you come out with your band and do it with us, and I will take care of the rest."

I said, "Peter, I don't know it well enough to sing any lead on the verses, just the chorus, okay?"

So I waited, and after about five songs I heard Peter say to the audience, "Are you ready to hear the coolest, hottest, best new band out of Georgia?"

Over ten thousand fans yelled back, "YEAH!"

"Let me introduce to you, then, my friend Caspar McCloud and his band Three!"

Now I really thought we were just going to help sing back–up on this song, but when I walked out on stage Jody Davis nodded to his tech to give me Peter's blue Gretch Guitar. I then found myself playing a song I had never played before in front of thousands of people. But Peter wasn't finished with me. Suddenly, he walked out of the spotlight and left me in it alone, soloing. It was the autumn of 1998, and a night I'll never forget. It was the last performance I was to have, for that very night I experienced serious heart trouble.

Out of Sync

A year before that Newsboys concert, I began having some heart problems and had my first ambulance ride to the hospital and a one–week stay. The treatment and counsel from the doctors seemed very unsatisfactory. So I, believing the Lord would heal me, signed myself out of the hospital and walked away in faith. I would not now tell anyone to do what I did, because it was just too dangerous. I had little understanding then of the situation—but I did have strong faith. Thankfully, the Lord in his mercy kept me going strong for another year until I fell back into the sin of fear that was behind my heart disease.

For God hath not given us the spirit of fear; but of power, and of love, and of a sound mind. II Timothy 1:7

Men's hearts failing them for fear, and for looking after those things which are coming on the earth: for the powers of heaven shall be shaken. Luke 21:26

Whilst in hospital, my friend David Z., a very talented musician and a devoted man of God, came to visit. David owned a recording studio and helped my band Three record our first CD, "In Our Lifetime," featuring some duets with Phil Keaggy. I had first met David a few years earlier at a Christian musicians' meeting. While we were all taking turns praying, the Lord spoke to my spirit and told me I should talk to this man. Later, I introduced myself and we became instant friends. David was different from most of the other Christian brothers and sisters I knew at the time. He was a Spirit–filled believer who laid hands on me just as they did in the book of Acts and prayed that I would be baptized in the Holy Ghost. I was. I received it by faith just like I had received salvation.[4]

4. See Appendix, Baptized in the Holy Spirit

Led by the Holy Spirit

After I was baptized in the Holy Ghost I started trying to explain to David an odd experience I was having. I was hearing a strange language in my head! David said that the Lord had given me a prayer language. He told me that when I didn't know what to pray or how to pray, the Holy Spirit would pray through me. "Go ahead and speak it out," he instructed me.

Perhaps you've been taught like I was: the gift of tongues along with all the other gifts of the Holy Spirit had passed away when the last Apostle died. So, before I took David's word for it, I telephoned my good friend, Seth Barnes of Adventures in Missions.

Seth was an elder in the church where I had been on staff in Florida, a brilliant man of God, and one of my most trusted friends. He always seemed to be one step ahead of me in discovering Bible truths. I told Seth what had happened and he assured me this was a gift from the Lord. Then he read Scriptures to back up what he was saying.

The next day was Sunday, and at the time we were attending an evangelical church in Atlanta that was home to thousands of believers. The pastor was a very good speaker and the church was on fire for the Lord. The pastor was also a good man, and I knew him and his family personally. What's more, he had a doctorate from an impressive theological school. His was a good church with lots of programs, and many people got saved there every week.

To digress a little, it always makes my eyes tear up when people come forward to accept Jesus Christ of Nazareth as their savior. Nothing in this world is more important than recognizing that you are a sinner, repenting and asking the Lord to forgive you. There is nothing you can do that is so bad [4]See Appendix, Baptized in the Holy Spirit

the Lord will not forgive you if you ask him. Jesus paid for your sins by being crucified and He shed His Holy blood to cover your sins and mine. If you go to any born–again Christian church and start asking questions, you will find it filled with people who did just that. They are people who did sinful things and got to the point where they recognized that they needed Jesus Christ to save them. He is absolutely the only way you can be saved.

"I am the way, the truth, and the life: no man cometh unto the Father, but by Me". (John 14:6)

"That if you shall confess with your mouth the Lord Jesus, and shall believe in your heart that God has raised Him from the dead, you shall be saved."(Romans 10:9)

Every Wind of Doctrine

So there I was, sitting in the morning service, when suddenly this pastor said, "Now I don't speak in tongues because Jesus did not speak in tongues." That sounded very good and very pious, and very knowledgeable. In response, thousands of people jumped to their feet and wildly applauded all at once. But I was grieved in my spirit by this display, and thought, "Wait a minute, tongues came after Pentecost! What are you people doing acting like a bunch of sheep following any wind of doctrine? Are we not told to test all things by the Spirit?"

When someone you trust gets something like this so wrong, you cannot help but question what else they may have taught you that is not lining up with the Holy Word of God. I ended up leaving that church a few months later and have since discovered that the Lord has placed a few Spirit–filled believers on staff and in that congregation. I pray that when the time is right, they can correct this pastor in all meekness and gentleness and instruct those believers who oppose themselves, and do as Scripture admonishes.

> *But foolish and unlearned questions avoid, knowing that they do gender strifes. And the servant of the Lord must not strive: but be gentle unto all men, apt to teach, patient, in meekness instructing those that oppose themselves: if God peradventure will give them repentance to the acknowledging of the truth: And that they may recover themselves out of the snare of the devil, who are taken captive by him at his will.*
> *(II Timothy 3:23–26)*

It is so amazing to me to read my Bible and see these truths—written about the Christian, not the unsaved!

Standing on Faith

One week after I was hospitalized, the band was scheduled to play at a large church. The leadership found out what had happened to me and was ready to cancel our concert. But I told them, "No, I will be fine. We will be there, God willing."

Well, I wasn't fine. We got there late, which complicated matters, and the youth pastor was upset. He wanted me to play acoustically to avoid wasting time setting up the band equipment. What's more, friends of mine were in the audience and I worried about disappointing them. Suddenly, my heart started pounding. I did not want anyone to ever be upset with me, or my ministry.

Contrary to what Jesus admonished, I was afraid of what people would think. Back then, integrity—which was a source of pride for me—meant everything. I have undergone such a radical transformation that today I don't really care what anyone thinks of me. I only care about what God thinks, and I know he loves me. He knew me before the foundations of the world were laid.

Well, we set up our instruments anyway, electric and loud! The youth loved it—even if some of the leaders weren't so sure. I had played solo there the year before, and I preached as well. The Holy Spirit had given me a message that turned many lives around, with close to 100 decisions for the Lord.

But this night was difficult, both spiritually and physically. After the concert, Dr. Kerry Severin, a dear friend, pushed his way through the throng of kids wanting autographs. I took Kerry's hand and placed it over my heart. His face turned grave at what he felt, and immediately he got me away from the crowd. He led me into a back room, grabbed the leadership and commanded them to pray.

It was the first time I had ever left my guitar for someone else to pack up. But somehow, guitars and other material things don't matter when you are wondering if you will live through the night.

Actually my heart problems had been going on for years, but they never lasted very long. So I ignored the symptoms. The first time I remember really being in trouble was on a Friday afternoon, the day the first Three CD was going to the mastering plant. My heart started pounding but I carried on, thinking it would go back to normal soon.

Six hours later, since the pounding continued, I rang up my doctor's office and spoke to a nurse. She sounded very concerned and asked me to get someone to drive me to the urgent care facility.

Reluctantly, I awakened Joan and off we went. The doctor who examined me gave me some pills he said would slow my heart down, and sent me home. No sooner had we gotten there than the telephone rang. The Newsboys wanted me to come do a concert the next day. I assured them I would be there, hung up the phone, and passed out. The medicine had kicked in, and now my heart wasn't pumping fast enough. I never showed up for the concert.

Joan found me and called for an ambulance. I was kept in the hospital for a week until I again signed myself out. (The same admonishment goes here: I don't advise anyone to do what I've done!) And about a year later, at another Newsboys concert where I played a solo, it happened yet again. This time, I found myself feeling like I was still rocking–out on stage hours after the concert ended. And what followed was another ambulance ride. This time, instead of fighting it, I just gave up, deciding there was nothing I could do but trust in God.

Whether we live or die, we are the Lord's and it is in him we trust. So I stopped thinking about my career and all the things I wanted to accomplish. Lying on that stretcher, my mind wandered and I noticed a spider web on the ceiling of the ambulance. I remember wondering why they hadn't cleaned it up—seeing as how they are supposed to be concerned about those things. And just then, the medic—who was on the phone with the hospital—announced that my heart had suddenly gone back into a normal sinus rhythm. Praise God!

A Sobering Prognosis

Doctors diagnosed two heart diseases. The first, called atrial fibrillation, is a permanent condition in which the heart beats unevenly and very rapidly—as much as 200 to 300 beats per minute (a normal rate is 60 to 100). Any type of increased stress, including performing for an audience, causes an adrenaline surge which can send the heart into this abnormal beat which, in turn, can cause a stroke or heart attack. The other disease, mitral valve prolapse, is a condition in which the blood leaves the heart and immediately flows back in to it.

I kept on believing I was going to be healed, but I also started seeing a cardiologist who put me on a lot of medication. My best hope, he said, was to drastically change my lifestyle. Give up performing. Give up horses. Stay away from any physical exertion. And stay on a rotation of drugs that would either keep me alive or kill me. As I came to find out later, one of the drugs he recommended had been shown to cause death in half of the people who took it! But at that time, it seemed I had no other choice. My plans ruined and dreams dashed, I spent time and money going from one specialist to another looking for a different answer. In a state of despair, I cried out to God. "Lord, you are still healing all these other people; please heal me as well!"

After one traumatic doctor's visit, I remember talking on the telephone with Phil Keaggy and bursting into tears. I could hardly get the words out. I felt alone, abandoned and afraid. Phil didn't panic because he knew exactly what to do. He prayed earnestly for a calm in my spirit. Immediately, an amazing sense of peace came over me. I knew there was a simple answer. I still had to just trust in God.

The pastors and church people who learned about my illness were almost as bad as the doctors. They offered sympathy but no hope, as if to say, "It's okay for you to ask God to heal a cold, but don't ask for anything too big," as though God is not doing miracles anymore. Yet,

Scripture reveals how much Jesus actually took on himself with regard to both our physical and spiritual states:

Surely he has borne our griefs (literally, sickness) and carried our sorrows (literally, pains): Yet we did esteem him stricken, smitten of God, and afflicted. But he was wounded for our transgressions, he was bruised for our iniquities: the chastisement of our peace was upon Him; and with His stripes (physical wounds) we are healed. (Romans 5:1)

Spiritually, Jesus took our punishment for our sins and iniquities that we might have peace with God Almighty. And physically he bore our sicknesses and pains so we might be healed through his wounds. Matthew 8:16–17 records that Jesus healed all the sick so that this word (taken from Isaiah) might be fulfilled. We can sum it up this way: Jesus was punished that we might be forgiven and his body was broken that we might be healed.

While in the hospital again from yet another episode, I phoned up a pastor friend seeking comfort. But all he succeeded in doing was making matters worse by telling me that my incurable heart disease was actually good news, something for which to be thankful. His reasoning was that I would go to be with the Lord before "the rest of us." It wasn't what I wanted to hear and contained no comfort at all. I had a wife and had two children to look after. What would become of them?

Finding a Miracle or Two

Then something happened to change things completely. I soon found myself being shepherded by a pastor–friend whose church was about an hour's drive from my home. He showed me what the Bible teaches about healing, prayed for me and sent me home with a number of books. One contained a story about a child in Wales from the year 1303. The account takes place at Conwy Castle, which happens to be one of my favorite castles to visit. One night, a child named Roger fell 28 feet to his death off the bridge by the castle wall. He was not discovered until morning. The Lord used a man named John Syward to raise the child from the dead.[5]

This was proof that God was still doing miracles more than a thousand years after the last Apostle passed away—even though many churches teach against it. What's more, II Corinthians 1:20 says *that all the promises of God in him (Christ) are yea, and in him, amen, unto the glory of God by us;* and isn't Jesus the same yesterday, today and forever? *Malachi 3:6, "For I am the Lord, I change not."*

But I still wasn't convinced. I pleaded with God that if this really were true, would he please tell me through another witness. Straightway, I checked my e-mail and it was there waiting for me. My friend Seth Barnes had sent me the account of a girl named Rosa in Mozambique, where poverty and mortality rates are startlingly high. A pastor there came across the dead body of Rosa and began to pray. And pray. And pray. He kept it up for not one day or two days, but for three entire days. Miraculously, God raised Rosa from the dead.

Seth's e-mail ended with an encouragement to just believe—nay sayers could go to Mozambique and meet Rosa themselves. I couldn't go to Mozambique, but I did phone Seth straightway and started asking questions. Seth assured me he had heard a number of stories such as this and referred me to a book by Jack Deere about an evangelist in Zaire who raised a child from the dead. Within the story was a copy of the death certificate, dated 1985. News of this miracle spread throughout the city, and that weekend more than 200,000 people came to hear the Gospel preached. Many were saved and many were healed. I began to believe that even if I were to die from heart trouble, God could still heal me—or bring me back from the dead!

This simple act of faith, which I humbly compare to Jesus' statement in John 20:29, *"Because thou hast seen Me, thou hast believed: blessed are they that have not seen, and yet have believed,"* was the turning point in my life. I decided I would choose to believe God. Nothing is impossible with Him.

I had been reading a number of Derek Prince's books, as well as some by Charles and Frances Hunter. I was convinced that somehow the Lord would deliver me out of this dreadful mess, but I did not know how or when. During a subsequent doctor's visit, arrangements were being made to place me in a hospital so they could monitor a change in medication. The Lord sent me a Christian nurse, and when I started telling her about all the stories that I had read about modern day miracles she looked at me and said, "This new medicine is much worse than what you are on now. If I were you, if you truly believe the Lord, I would run away from this office as quickly as you can. Run to the Lord—only he can really heal you!"

I got up and told the receptionist that I had changed my mind and asked her to cancel my hospital stay. Then I left before they could stop me. Except for the Lord, I was finally out of options.

Looking back now at myself—a man who was very sick and nearly without hope—I realize there were places in my life as a believer that the Devil had taken me captive at his will. I desperately needed someone who could show me the errors of my ways—someone sent of the Lord to minister the truth. There I was, a born–again, spirit–filled believer struggling with sin issues. What terrible sins had I committed? I was afraid of dying! Do you realize that is a sin?

The Lord tells us over and over again, "Fear not." Why should any believer be afraid to die? Where will we go? I had no doubt I would be with the Lord in heaven, but I was still afraid to die. Who do you suppose was helping me stay afraid and hopeless? It certainly wasn't the Lord!

5. From *Surprised by the Power of the Spirit*, by Jack Deere, Grand Rapids, Michigan Zondervan Publishing House

Don't Despise Prophecy

Soon after I made that decision to simply put my trust in God, I was attending the church service of a friend of mine, Pastor Eddie Rogers. He brought up my name in the middle of his sermon and started praying for me. I did not realize that he was also prophesying. My friend Donna Saylors later transcribed the tape of the service and e—mailed me the following. The date was December 10, 2000.

"For the Lord says, 'Long life and length of days I will give you. Long life and length of days I will give you. For even now I'm falling upon you. Make plans for the future, for you are my servant in the palm of my hand. Before you were ever formed, fashioned in your mother's womb, I had a plan for you and your destiny. Your destiny is yet to be fulfilled. But I give peace right now—a foretaste—by telling you long life and length of days is your portion. Totally healed, you'll be a miracle. You'll be a miracle to your doctors. You'll be a miracle to your cardiologist. A miracle!'"

Yet, there was a lingering doubt, or perhaps a certain impatience. I had come to the point where I asked, "How many times must I pray and be prayed for? How many times must I be anointed with oil and have elders and pastors lay hands on me, and still I am not healed? Where is God in all of this? Why are others getting healed and I am still waiting?" There had to be an answer somewhere; something was missing in my understanding. Seth told me it was right to keep going forward in church to be healed. "Keep asking," he said. "Keep pressing in. Keep searching for the Lord and you will find him."

I once drove about 14 hours with Seth to hear a minister who was claiming many healings. I was very disappointed. There was a lot of manipulation going on in the service; they brought up people who said they sowed a thousand dollars in faith money and got $100,000 back. There were stories of people giving and God repaying the favor with a brand new Cadillac. Then the minister started praying for people and pushing them down. He prayed for me and knocked me off–balance so I would fall.

After the service, three very large men appeared and beckoned to me. Apparently, I was to be escorted to a back room to meet with the minister. I was pleasantly surprised. But once in the room, this minister confronted me, asking why I had come. When I told him I simply wanted to be healed, he started shouting at me and said things a minister would never, or should never, say.

I was very confused and hurt. He had apparently mistaken me for someone else, but even so, it was a nasty thing to do to anyone, especially to a heart patient. Seth asked me what happened and I would not say a word. I did not speak against God's anointed. Do you believe a man of God may start out right, but then fall way off course?

The next day Pastor Eddie (who had prophesied that I would live a full life) telephoned me and told me he knew all about it. The three huge fellows had been as shocked as I was; apparently, they thought the minister was going to pray for me. Instead he "blessed" me right out of there. Still, I kept on believing I would find God somewhere, and when I did he would heal me.

A More Excellent Way

Hebrews 11 tells us that faith is the substance of things hoped for, the evidence of things not seen. I would soon be living proof of that, and Pastor Henry Wright of Pleasant Valley Church in Thomaston,

Georgia would be God's chosen instrument. It was the year 2000 and a guitar student of mine named Libby Hebdon brought me a book. She knew of my health issues and wanted me to read Pastor Wright's book about the spiritual roots of disease. I politely read a few lines. For some reason I just didn't connect with it.

Then a few weeks later, my wife and I were at a party where an acquaintance named Ronald Barfield started telling me how his wife got healed at a place called Pleasant Valley Church. He gave me the phone number. At this point, I was ready. Taking all sorts of dangerous medicines daily, and reeling from the horrendous side effects, I was looking for even a glimmer of hope and I gave Henry Wright a call. Somehow, I had miscopied the number and had to call Information. Unbeknownst to me, instead of getting the church listing I got the pastor's home phone number. Imagine my surprise when Henry himself, a man who spent most of his time on the road ministering to people all over the country (indeed, the world), answered the phone! I just sort of blurted out, "Hello, my name is Caspar and I was diagnosed with A–fib."

Pastor Wright has been ministering to people with disease since the early 1980s. And I have personally seen many people get healed of all sorts of physical, emotional and spiritual ailments through his ministry. But at the time I first spoke to him, I knew next to nothing about the man and his ministry—nothing about the spiritual roots of disease and why certain people get specific diseases. That's why Pastor Wright's first comment came as such a shock.

"Caspar, you are probably a very sensitive guy who is an artist or musician, right?"

I almost dropped the telephone. How could he know that from what I just said?

"Have you had any miracles at your church?" I inquired. He responded that, yes, they had seen quite a few. (I found out later that there have been thousands.) And he also told me that God's perfect will was not to heal me. *His perfect will is that I don't get sick!*

We spoke for a few more minutes and he invited me to come see him. I wasted no time and began investigating this ministry. I ordered his book and began reading. It was amazing how what he said bore witness with my spirit. Halfway through the book, I felt the Holy Spirit urging me to give Henry a call. Immediately! I did, and we had another interesting conversation. I don't often meet someone who has his insights, compassion and love. He asked me very tough questions and gave me several Scriptures, including this one that promises God still heals:

> *If thou wilt diligently hearken to the voice of the LORD thy God, and wilt do that which is right in his sight, and wilt give ear to his commandments, and keep all his statutes, I will put none of these diseases upon thee, which I have brought upon the Egyptians: for I am the LORD that healeth thee. (Exodus 15:26)*

Diagnosing a Spirit of Fear

Soon afterwards, I stood face to face with Pastor Henry Wright. We went into his office with his associate pastor, Anita Hill, who was a nurse and has her own amazing testimony of healing. After about two minutes I decided that I could trust these people with my life. There was a holiness about them that I had seen before in very few people, Phil Keaggy being one. Once again, I felt like the Lord was looking right at me through their eyes.

Pastor Henry again started asking me very tough questions about my life. And I felt the freedom to tell him anything he wanted to know. Both Pastor Henry and Anita shared with me personal things about their past that helped put me at ease. Several other verses they shared seemed to neatly sum up my life:

Hope deferred maketh the heart sick. (Proverbs 13:12)

For God did not give us a spirit of fear, but of power, love and a sound mind… (II Timothy 1:7)

Thoughts From Pastor Henry Wright

Sometimes we don't understand disease like we need to because we don't see the connection between our spirituality, psychology and biology. But it's right there in the Word of God, and it can also be seen in the study of science.

We are spiritual beings that have a soul, or psyche, and live in physical bodies. I call this the missing link because many times we forget that we are a spirit. There is a connection between our thoughts and our health— between our spirituality and our health. Even science knows the connection between fear, anxiety and stress and specific diseases. It's taught in medical schools.

The manifestation of the disease often indicates a problem on the spiritual level. Caspar's atrial fibrillation was an arrhythmic problem considered by the medical community and the journals of medicine to be a stress disorder. However, few doctors ever discuss the issues of thoughts or spirituality with heart patients. And so the patients go into various types of disease management and all types of things to try to bring that heart back into balance.

So when Caspar called me and said, "Atrial fibrillation," I knew him. I knew him because of my study of the foundation of the spirituality and the psychology of many diseases. I knew his battle and I knew his enemy. People who come under stress—at the severe level that produces this degree of disease—are often very compassionate and sensitive. People that have sensitive hearts come down under things more quickly than people with hard hearts, yet people with hard hearts end up with other diseases caused by their hardness of heart. So which is worse: to have a soft heart or a hard heart? Both are wrong.

You can have compassion, but sometimes the enemy uses that as leverage to cause us to go down under things. We become introspective and begin to "stew in our stuff." We begin to have a fear of man, a fear of what could go wrong and a fear of failure.

I remember saying to Caspar, "Well, let's see...atrial fibrillation...you must be a sensitive individual, and maybe in the arts or a professional musician." And all of that was true. The next thing I told him was equally shocking: that his disease was not an accident. He didn't get nailed out of the blue. He had fear, anxiety and stress.

Caspar had become an enemy to himself and didn't even know it. These thoughts, feelings and sensitivities had been transposed into a disease. And so I took him on a journey into the Scriptures, specifically II Timothy 1:7, which says that God has not given us the spirit of fear, but power, love and a sound mind. I told him that his falling into a lack of power, love and soundness of mind indicated that he had "become one" with an invisible spirit of fear.

Well, if I remember correctly, that astounded him. Most people do not think there's any connection between their spirituality and disease because we are programmed by Jungian psychotherapy principles to think that this is just a soul problem—an inner–healing problem.

Caspar's soul and his long–term memory (his spirit) had "become one" with fear. He could not separate himself from this spirit of fear in his own thoughts. And so he had gone down under it. As a result, heart disease, allergies and asthma were produced in his life. Allergies are the result of a compromised immune system caused by too much cortisol. Cortisol, the "fight or flight" steroid is naturally released in times of fear, stress and anxiety. However, it is meant for short—term use only. Long—term, it destroys the immune system and allergies are often the result.

The Bible says, "Take no thought for tomorrow, the evil of today is sufficient unto itself." God did not intend for us to live with fear. Perfect love casts out fear. And if we haven't been loved perfectly, we can go under fear and lose our peace.

Caspar had other diseases including mitral valve prolapse, which is listed in the medical journals as a stress disorder, the result of an imbalance of the sympathetic nervous system. And asthma is also listed in the Journal of American Medicine as a stress disorder. We have found that asthma affects people who have a fear of abandonment. So our friend Caspar really was caught in a whirlwind, not just by one spirit of fear, but several. And they hit him from different angles with more than one disease.

Now these diseases were irritants in Caspar's life, but atrial fibrillation can kill you. It can cause cardiac arrest or elevated blood pressure, which can cause a stroke.

Caspar had gone into fear about tomorrow; he had a fear of failure, a fear of making mistakes, fear of rejection and a fear of man. All of these fears were attacking his body through his thoughts. Besides this, Caspar also had an enemy assigned to him for his destruction——literally assigned to kill him. It was a spirit of death that had joined him to remove him from this planet. And if he didn't succumb to it, it would keep him so messed up with fear and disease that he couldn't function in the desires of his heart. He's a musician and an artist, but even more, he is a husband and a father. And so Caspar had lost his peace. He was scared.

But then I gave Caspar some good news. I informed him he was not having a mental breakdown. This disease was the work of an evil spirit——in

91

fact, there was a spirit of fear working in him that was not a negative emotion or a psychological defect. An invisible being, a spirit of fear, had joined him.

In II Timothy 1:7, it clearly says that God has not given us a spirit of fear. It does not say God has not given us a negative emotion or a psychological defect. In Ephesians 6, Paul said that our battle, or our war, is not with flesh and blood or others or ourselves, but with principalities and powers and spiritual wickedness in high places. An evil spirit of fear programmed Caspar in his thinking and he didn't know it. I showed him that these thoughts, feelings and impressions that began to come at him and that produced disease were not really him.

Well, that opened him up to be able to understand that he had an intelligent enemy defined by the Bible. And that enemy had joined him to interfere with his life because it had a right to. We have given the enemy a legal right to plague us because we don't understand the source of our thoughts.

I began to disciple Caspar over the phone and load him up with every teaching tape known to man about this subject. And he began a journey of understanding how God thinks and what God has said. He began to awaken spiritually and to understand the Bible like he'd never understood it before. Caspar began to have discernment of invisible things and the enemy was not happy.

When Henry told me that fear can be a spirit, all the light bulbs went on in my head. We talked at length and he began uncovering the iniquities and unconfessed sins I had in my life. He asked me about my father. I told him something I had not talked about for 17 years: that my father had been murdered and I had been unable to attend the funeral. And if you'll remember, a close relative had blamed me for my father's death. Until the moment that I spoke with Henry, I had no idea of the effect that recrimination had had on my life.

I didn't want to discuss it with Henry, but the more I protested, the more obvious it became to both of us that this was something I had to deal with. I was able to see how this and the sins in my life were making me sick. As he ministered to me over the weeks and months, and as I worked on the spiritual issues of forgiving myself and asking God to heal my broken heart, I began to get well.

He had told me, "You are no longer fighting this battle alone; I am going to be fighting it right along side of you." Then he added, "I hate to lose to the devil. We are going to try and win this battle so you can get well and live."

When he said that, my eyes suddenly began to tear up. At that time I did feel abandoned. I felt alone and even shunned by my dear family and friends. Yet during this defining moment, it was like the Lord used Pastor Henry's body to hold me in his arms and infuse me with hope and comfort.

Yes, I knew the Lord was with me always, but I also felt he was somewhere far away. I finally realized he was not the one who had moved away. It was I. The Lord was the one who was holding me together, while I grew more and more distant as my heart disease got worse. But now everything had changed.

What changed, what really had changed? Pastor Henry had asked me a few direct and simple questions, one of which went something like this: after you got saved and the Lord in His grace and mercy washed you clean from all unrighteousness and forgave your every sin, how many sins did you continue in? All I could think was, "*Oops!*"

He showed me Proverbs 13:12, which says, "Hope deferred makes the heart sick, but when the desire comes, it is a tree of life." He also gave me the following verse that shows who my enemy truly is:

For we wrestle not against flesh and blood, but against principalities, against powers, against the rulers of the darkness of this world, against spiritual wickedness in high places. (Ephesians 6:12)

I started to understand. There are invisible, intelligent evil spirits that join forces and follow a hierarchy. Hebrews 12:15 says, "Looking diligently lest any man fail of the grace of God: lest any root of bitterness springing up trouble you, and thereby many be defiled."

Bitterness Reaps its Harvest

Yes, I had a spirit of bitterness. I blamed people in my past for ruining my music career. I was in sin and did not even know it! At first, I thought I was a good Christian—in good standing before the Lord. But once I started to unravel this mess, I discovered that I was even bitter against myself. That was a big one to deal with, too.

I learned that these evil spirits follow an order that goes from bad to worse. You begin in unforgiveness, which leads to resentment, which bears fruit in retaliation. Then anger steps in, then hatred and violence which, when it gives birth, is murder.

The Bible teaches that you can murder someone with your tongue. Is this the way God created us to behave? I recognized that these spirits were not me, but they had gained entry into my life. I had allowed evil thoughts in, beginning with unforgiveness. And when I allowed these thoughts, an evil spirit of bitterness joined itself to me.

This is what the Apostle Paul was talking about in Romans 7 where he admits that he doesn't do the things he wants to do, and the things he does not want to do, that is what he finds himself doing. Why? Because of the sin that dwells within.

94

I spent many weeks with a ministry team from Pleasant Valley working on areas in my past when I had participated with sin. One by one, I would renounce my transgressions before the Lord and ask for His forgiveness. Next, I had to accept his forgiveness (and also, forgive myself). The pastors would then ask me to look at them, and quietly, but with authority, they would cast out the evil spirit in the name of Jesus Christ of Nazareth.

At one point, we talked over the events of the day my father was murdered and then they cast out the evil spirits of self–pity, rejection and abandonment. I remember being fine all through the process until these unholy things were told to leave, whereupon I burst into tears. I asked them why I was crying so hard. Anita gently explained that sometimes evil spirits leave through our tears.

Here is a sample of those prayers—spoken out loud, so all the invisible spirits in both Kingdoms could hear as I prayed to my God:

Father God, I come before your throne, confessing that my feelings have been sinful. I did not know what to do about them before now. In the name of Jesus Christ of Nazareth, and as an act of my free will, I purpose and choose to forgive so–and–so from my heart. I forgive them for what they did and how they did it. And in the name of Jesus Christ of Nazareth, I cancel all their debts and obligations to me.

In the name of Jesus Christ of Nazareth, I break and cancel Satan's power over me in this memory, and all the resulting pain that came with it. I come out of agreement with the devil and his plans for me. I command all the tormentors that have been assigned to me because of my unforgiveness to leave me now in the name of Jesus Christ. Instead, I invite your Holy Spirit to come into my heart, and heal me of this pain.

Holy Spirit, please tell me your truth in this situation. (Here, I would wait and listen quietly and allow the Holy Spirit to speak to my heart.)

Thank you, Father God, that because of what your Son did for me by taking my place on the cross, all this is now possible.

Walking in Righteousness

The ministers at Pleasant Valley taught me eight important principles of walk–out, which is the process of keeping yourself in a place where you can "walk out" of the old ways and walk into righteousness. This is what you must do whenever you're confronted with evil in which you have participated:

The 8 R's:

1. **Recognize** when you have sinned. *Isaiah 5:13–14; Hosea 4:6; Hebrews 5:13–14; Jeremiah 3:15*
2. Take **Responsibility** for the sin. *Psalm 51:3–4; II Corinthians 3:18*
3. **Repent**. Ask God in the name of the Lord Jesus to forgive you for participating in the sin. Accept His forgiveness and then forgive yourself. *Acts 3; Revelation 2:16, 21–22, 3:3*
4. **Renounce**. Fall completely out of agreement with the sin and have a perfect hatred for it. *I Corinthians 10:20, 1 Samuel 15:22, Hosea 4:6*
5. **Remove** it; get rid of the thing in your life that is causing you to sin. *Ezekiel 18:30–32; John 3:16; Ezekiel 32*
6. **Resist** the devil. Stand against the sin and break the power of the memories in Jesus' name. *Luke 11:24–26; James 1:14–15*
7. **Rejoice**. Thank the Lord for every victory! *Isaiah 35:1–10*
8. **Restore** others in the faith; build them up. *Psalm 51:12; Isaiah 58:10–12; 42: 22*

I cannot tell you how many times a day I had to go over this list. But just like they said it got easier as I continued "walking out." I practiced thinking about what I was thinking about!

But even so, every morning and evening I would still have to take this awful medicine for my heart. It would slow my heart down and would slow me down as well. I was at a point where I could hardly even carry my guitar. Every day for two years I would thank the Lord and proclaim that I would be completely healed.

The day finally came when I needed a doctor to wean me off the medicines. So I began seeing Dr. Terri Allen of the Fit Center in Montgomery, Alabama, who has since become like a sister to me. We had a mutual interest in horses, and I discovered that she actually had worked with Mahesh Chavda, the pastor from Jack Deere's book. She knew all about the miracles and added more details. I was amazed how the Lord was always behind the scenes, orchestrating so many events!

Dr. Terri began treatments, which included bringing up my magnesium levels—depleted because of stress, which further complicated my heart condition. During one of these treatments, I had a visit from my friend Jim Ousley, who raised my horse as a yearling and was keeping him for me. He stopped in on his way to Florida. I was hooked up to an IV and he just sat awhile with me. I knew I looked in bad shape at the time.

Finally, Jim summoned up the courage to ask me a very difficult question. He said that some people had been inquiring about my horse. Since I could not ride anymore, could they buy him? My eyes started to tear up and Jim quickly said we'd wait awhile longer. He proclaimed that he believed the Lord could heal me and that I would ride my horse again.

The first time I went to see Dr. Terri at her office, she found out about my horse and the pronunciation made by my cardiologist that

I would never be able to ride again. After the day's treatment, Dr. Terri told me we were going to her farm and that I had to break off the curse spoken over me. So we did. I rode one of her horses, and it was a milestone in my life.

It took a year of IV treatments and care by Dr. Terri to get me weaned off all heart medicine. But finally, the day came when I was completely free and we decided to celebrate. Dr. Terri and her mother agreed to meet me at Pleasant Valley Church for their Friday night service.

God Performs a Miracle for Me

Dr. Terri, her mother and I arrived at Pleasant Valley Church on July 3, 2001. It felt great to be playing guitar in the praise band. My thoughts were filled with praise for God, because he had healed my sick heart. I was no longer on dangerous heart medicine. I was feeling great and very thankful.

When I arrived in the sanctuary that day, some of the members of the praise team found out I was to be playing later on in the service. They quickly came to ask if I would not mind sitting in with the band since I was already there. Not knowing any of the music they had planned to play, and always up for a chance to share my gifts and see if I could improvise my way through, I agreed.

Now I must tell you that a service at Pleasant Valley can last more than a few hours, depending on how the Holy Spirit directs it. Pleasant Valley Church follows the model established in I Corinthians 14:

How is it then, brethren? When ye come together, every one of you hath a psalm, hath a doctrine, hath a tongue, hath a revelation, hath an interpretation. Let all things be done unto edifying.

There is no order of service at Pleasant Valley. The staff simply gathers to pray before they begin, and then they ask the Holy Spirit to take over. Anything may happen after this point. So there is much freedom to let the Holy Spirit direct the music; it often seems that the Spirit has woven it into a masterpiece of prophecy. That day, we could sense a powerful anointing in the place.

After a few songs, my heart started to act oddly. I recall thinking this can't be happening—I am healed of this heart problem! I had been off all medications now for exactly one week. But while we were worshipping the Lord, I realized I was in trouble. I began debating what I should do. How could I get Pastor Henry's attention in the middle of leading worship?

Just then, there was an audible voice in my head that sounded more like someone speaking into my ear. It said quite clearly, "If you get off the altar now you won't get healed." "Wait!" I thought, "God wouldn't say that to me because I am already healed!"

At the same time, according to several witnesses from the church, a new sound began filling the air. One of my friends in the praise band looked over because he heard something amazing on the guitar and he thought it was me playing! But at that time, I was leaning against a pillar, looking white as a ghost. Yet strange, celestial music was filling the room, joining the sounds of the praise band and the congregation singing.

The Battle for My Life

I was aware of the sound that had enveloped us, but I was also aware of my heart not working properly, which captured most of my attention and concern. At that point, I laid my guitar down on the floor and walked off the stage. I was feeling horribly weak and almost collapsed as I headed toward the chair next to Dr. Terri. She knew something was terribly wrong. Pastor Henry looked over at me and started to say, "Caspar," but stopped. We made eye contact. I saw him mouth the words, "I will deal with you later, brother."

Pastor Henry has this amazing gift of discernment: when he looks into your eyes, it's almost like he is looking into your soul. I have seen him do that to people and tell them what disease they are dealing with. He can "read their mail" without ever having met them and he seems to be always correct. How? The Holy Spirit reveals it.

As he began teaching, I was busy! I was praying and waging battle. By his stripes I am healed! I refuse to fear! Okay, what is the worst thing that can happen? I will die and go be with the Lord and on the day of resurrection I will get a new glorified body!

Thoughts From Pastor Henry Wright

Caspar had come and he'd joined our little worship band with his guitar and was singing alone, when all of a sudden he became very ill. He was disoriented and he wanted to sit down. And what's really interesting about this story is that he was under a doctor's care—in fact she was there with him! At the end of the service, she brought him up to me for prayer.

Now at this point, Caspar felt he had dealt with his issues. His heart arrhythmia was gone and he was under a doctor's care and had come off his medication. I don't recommend anybody coming off medication or leaving the protocol of disease management prescribed by a doctor. We always recommend withdrawal with a doctor's oversight. In this case, Caspar did have that oversight from his doctor. And now he was experimenting to see if we had truly gotten rid of the root issues.

Caspar was in "walk—out," beginning to take his life back. Now, there are two parts to walk—out. If there was a spirit of fear that had trained him to produce this disease in his thoughts, even if we remove the spirit of fear, Caspar's long—term memory would not have changed. And memory recall could trigger the same thing. The Bible's very clear that we are to have a renewal of our minds by the washing of the water of the Word. What word did Caspar need to renew his mind?

II Timonthy 1:7 — God has not given us the spirit of fear.

Psalm 34 — They called upon the name of the Lord and he delivered them of all of their fears.

Caspar believed this and had had a heart change. So why did he suddenly have heart trouble again? It seems to me the enemy came to interfere with his walk—out. The Bible says that when the evil spirit is cast out, it wanders through a dry place seeking a place of rest, and, finding none, it comes back to its original house to see if the house is filled or empty. This is probably a good example of what happened here. The spirit of fear and the spirit of death did not want to let Caspar go. They had a vested interest in his destruction and they had spent years developing a case to make him sick.

Thoughts From Dr. Terri Allen

I had been watching Caspar as he played that night, and I knew something was wrong. He became increasingly fidgety and then finally *left the stage. When he sat down he was very, very pale, his skin cool and clammy. I reached over to take his pulse. His heart was racing and irregular. After a while he felt a little better, but I suggested he talk to Pastor Henry at the end of the service and ask for prayer.*

In my mind, I knew there was a chance Caspar could have a heart attack, or throw a blood clot and have a stroke. But to voice my concerns would have increased Caspar's anxiety, which would increase the adrenaline. So we stayed very calm and prayed. After the service ended and people began to leave, Caspar and I walked over to Pastor Henry to ask for prayer. As he began speaking with us, Caspar began to get wobbly. I reached over to support his elbow and was joined on the other side by Pastor Anita Hill, who also happened to be a nurse. Caspar grew paler and paler. But we weren't ready for what happened next.

Thoughts From Caspar

I didn't know what was happening to me. I remember speaking to Henry, feeling faint and absolutely washed out. He was talking to me, but I couldn't comprehend him. I have a vague recollection of falling and Henry running around the pulpit—or perhaps what I remember is only what the witnesses told me.

Thoughts From Dr. Terri Allen

Before we could stop him, Caspar slipped out of our hands and fell to the floor.

At that moment, I knew we weren't just in a battle for Caspar's health; it was a battle for his life. Pleasant Valley Church is in a farmland area. The hospital was miles away and there was nothing to do but monitor Caspar's pulse. So Anita and I dropped down on either side and we each grabbed a wrist. And looking at each other across Caspar's fallen body, we shared the same startling knowledge. There was no pulse.

102

Thoughts From Pastor Henry Wright

There we were, standing over Caspar's body. Standing between life and death. What then? Should we have called 9–1–1? Jeremiah 33:3 says "Call unto me and I will answer you and I will show you great and mighty things that you have not known." Just then, the Spirit of God dropped into my heart and I knew that a spirit of death had taken Caspar out. It was like the enemy said, "Yeah, you think you're going to believe in God? Look what I can do."

The Bible says when the enemy comes in like a flood the spirit of God shall raise a standard against the enemy. All I can say is, I'm glad God has taught me spiritual things, because if not, I'd have been reaching for the phone to call 9–1–1. Yet by the time the ambulances arrived, Caspar would have been gone for a very long while.

I remember looking down at Caspar and saying, "Ah, I know what's happening here. I know what this is." Then I spoke to that invisible kingdom of evil, "Your problem is not with him anymore, you've got a problem with me." And in the gift of faith, I turned and addressed an invisible spirit of death in the name of Jesus and commanded it to loose Caspar and come out of him.

Thoughts From Caspar

The next thing I knew, I was looking up at Henry's wife Donna, saying, "What happened?"

Dr. Terry replied, "That, my dear brother, was spiritual warfare."

I have been told that as my pulse returned, Dr. Terri jumped back in complete astonishment. She asked Henry how he got my heart started and Pastor Henry replied, "I did not do that! God did that!"

Thoughts From Dr. Terri Allen

When Caspar's pulse returned it was quite intense. I remember commenting that the pulse pushed my fingers up off his wrist. The pulse was then in a totally normal rhythm and stayed there the 20 or 30 minutes that Anita and I continued monitoring him.

When the heart pauses like it did, it's sitting there with a lot of blood in the chambers and that puts a stretch on the fibers. It's not unknown that when the heart begins to beat again that you have a very intense contraction. At that point, Caspar's heart was converted from an abnormal rhythm of an atrial fibrillation to a normal sinus rhythm. That was nearly two years ago and Caspar has not been in an irregular heart rate or rhythm since that day. I do believe that God heals and he can sovereignly touch people. In the moment when Caspar's heart paused God really did something.

Thoughts From Caspar

I've been told that as Pastor Henry cast the spirit of death out of me, I began to writhe on the floor. This continued for several minutes until my body stopped convulsing and I rested peacefully for another 20 to 30 minutes.

Thoughts From Pastor Henry Wright

The Bible says the believer shall cast out devils. That's almost unfashionable to say in Christianity today. But for Caspar, it was not unfashionable. If I did not know that a Believer could cast out devils in the name of Jesus, would we have Caspar with us today? How much of the Bible do we not practice because we don't believe? I want to challenge all Christians to begin to think again and read the Bible and believe.

When I cast the spirit of death out of Caspar, his pulse returned instantly, so strongly that it knocked his doctor's thumb right off his wrist. And when that happened, he opened his eyes and we had Caspar back. We helped him up off the floor and he was well.

That was more than three years ago and his testimony has stood the test of time. Caspar has been examined by his doctor on several occasions. There have been no evidences of arrhythmia of the heart, no evidence of atrial *fibrillation coming back. And what's really neat about this testimony is that Caspar came back alive <u>and well</u>. God had healed him of all of his diseases. He no longer had mitral valve prolapse, asthma, or allergies. Psalm 34 had been fulfilled in his life. The Lord truly came and delivered him from all of his fears. And for that, God gets all of the glory.*

I'm reminded of a Scripture in Isaiah 13. "But my people have gone into captivity because they have no knowledge." The knowledge that we have in this area is so necessary for mankind. How many more people have we lost to a spirit of death and disease because we don't understand the pathways to health and disease?

When someone drops dead, it is the spirit of death. Some people might not agree that it was the spirit of death we were dealing with here. But the word of God tells us, beginning in I Corinthians 15:24, that when the end comes he shall have put down all rule and all authority and power. And the last enemy that shall be destroyed is death.

Jesus himself cast out spirits by laying hands on the people that came to him. I was following his example. I had the knowledge, and tools (gifts of the Holy Spirit), and anointing to do that. (As every man hath received the gift, even so minister the same one to another, as good stewards of the manifold grace of God. I Peter 4.10)

Caspar was a Christian when he first came to see me, but he also had a spirit of fear, a spirit of infirmity and a spirit of death.

Some people might disagree and say Caspar didn't really die at that moment. Well, I have one question for them. How long do you have to be dead before you're dead? Is it one minute? Two minutes? Five? Ten? Behind Caspar's disease was an evil spirit. And even if we had called 911 and they had been able to get his heart started again, Caspar would not have had the complete healing that he experienced.

"Now he which stablisheth us with you in Christ, and hath anointed us, is God; who hath also sealed us, and given the earnest of the Spirit in our hearts." (II Cor. 1:21, 22)

"He who believes in Me, the works that I do he will do also; and greater works then these he will do, because I go to My Father." (John 14:12)

Thoughts From Caspar

Finally, Dr. Terri and Anita helped me up. I stayed at Pleasant Valley's retreat center that night, and within a couple of days I felt ready to do what I was asked to do in the first place: give my testimony and play some songs I had written.

I walked into the sanctuary that night for the evening service and I was feeling a bit uneasy, so I asked my friend Scott Harper to pray with me. We walked over together to the place near the pulpit where, only a few days ago, I was lying without a pulse. Scott prayed and we reclaimed the area for the Lord, and gave thanks for my miraculous healing.

After the praise band played a while, it was my turn to speak and play. I decided I would play first and talk afterwards. I picked up my guitar and made myself ready for the first song. Suddenly the metal button that holds the guitar strap pulled out, which had never happened to me before or since. I caught my instrument before it fell to the floor. Stunned by this, I looked up and said, "Well, I suppose now I will have to play strapless," which got a big laugh and broke the tension I was feeling. After that, I calmly gave my testimony.

Epilogue

It has now been more than four years since that amazing night that I was healed in July 2001. I've never felt better. My strength has returned and I'm able to ride my horse for hours, lift heavy objects, and perform in front of an audience without feeling a bit sick. My heart has been rechecked by a doctor, who says it is as healthy as that of an 18–year–old.[6]

So what happened? Is the church today willing to accept that nothing is impossible with God? What about you? Mark 16 says signs and wonders follow those who believe. If signs and wonders are not following us, why not? Maybe we don't really believe. Maybe we have gotten off track somewhere. I was in sin by being in fear of the doctors' reports. Whose report are you going to believe? I will believe the Lord's!

Before Pastor Henry showed me by the Holy Scriptures that I was sinning, I lived in ignorance and the devil tried to kill me—in a church service! Imagine: there I was in church, serving my Lord and the devil tried to steal my life. How many others think they are immune to that evil kingdom because they are in church, serving God? If there is any area of sin that you're just trying to ignore, you crucify Christ all over again. We need to get saved, and stay that way. We need sanctification.

Thousands of people worldwide are now healthy, and marriages are restored and people's broken lives are mended, because Pastor Henry dedicated his life to serve God and help people recover themselves out of the snare of the devil. His ministry began when prayer alone was not working. So Henry went before the Lord and asked why. And the Lord began showing him the pathways of disease. I urge you, dear reader, to get a copy of his book, *A More Excellent Way*, and read every page.

Now that I have shared with you things from my heart—and you can sense him touching your heart—I have one thing left to say.

Now is the appointed time for you; today is the day of Salvation. Why not begin your own relationship with Jesus Christ this minute? Talk to your papa God right now and admit that you're a sinner. Ask him to forgive you for all the sins you have committed. Tell him that you're willing to turn away from your sins and receive Jesus as your Savior and Lord. Get in the habit of practicing the 8 R's.

Now thank him! You are a new creature in Christ, created for good works. If you said that prayer, please contact Pleasant Valley Church (800–453–5775) and tell them. They will help you connect with a local body of believers near you.

Or contact:
Disease Anonymous
800–342–5604

Or:
H2H Ministries
Website www.house2house.net

---

6. See Appendix for Doctor's statements

Appendix A

Teaching on Translations

When I was on staff with the church in West Palm Beach, Florida, I sometimes ended up ministering in music along with Dr. Charles Ryrie of the Ryrie Study Bible fame. Imagine that—Mister Hard Rock–and–Roll ministering alongside a professor from Dallas Theological Seminary! Actually, Dr. Ryrie was very supportive of my ministry and autographed and sent me many of his books to read. Once when we worked together, a man afterwards started debating me, strongly defending the authenticity of the King James Version and decrying the so–called vagaries of the New International Version (NIV). But he did not really explain his position. He just wanted to argue that he was right and we were wrong. Years later, I came to understand the reasoning behind the debate. I then did my own research and would like to give you a simple overview.

Back in the 1600's, when King James authorized the first English translation, he chose 51 Bible scholars, who, by the time of its completion, were reduced to 47. These scholars were put into six groups: two at Oxford, two at Cambridge, and two at Westminster. Any member of the clergy in England was allowed to oversee any and all translations being made from the Greek and Hebrew. They used the Antioch manuscript (Antioch was a place of refuge for the first persecuted saints) and when they finished, the Authorized King James Version of the Bible came into being. Tremendous revival resulted from this magnificent translation, with signs and wonders following.

In 1881 the Church of England allowed a revision of the King James Bible to update obsolete spelling and punctuation. Along came two men named Dr. Westcott and Dr. Hort, who instead pushed for big changes. They based their work on a faulty Syrian manuscript of dubious origin that was found in Egypt. (Isn't it interesting that Egypt always represented evil in the Bible? No offence to my Egyptian friends, as the Lord loves everyone.) The result is that all the modern English translations are now based on these two men's work.

Red flags should have gone up, but didn't. Both men were members of "The Ghostly Guild," a society whose purpose was to investigate ghostly appearances and other supernatural phenomena—the pursuit of which Scripture labels spiritism, a practice that is expressly forbidden in the Word of God. This is merely the most obvious danger sign. Other issues came up, but were ignored as well. Here are just a few: Westcott and Hort did not believe in miracles, nor in heaven, nor in the infallibility of the Bible, nor in the atoning work of Jesus Christ on the cross. They did believe in Purgatory and in the efficacy of prayers for the dead. They were drawn to Darwinism and hated everything about democracy. And yet, in the 21st Century, we read and study Bibles translated from a shadowy, unauthenticated text introduced by these two men.

Why have we never heard these things? Why is it not common knowledge that all modern translations of the Bible are not based on the original, authentic Masoretic texts but a version of the Holy Scriptures that is not authenticated? It appears very few people, laymen or pastors, are even aware of this. But instead of taking my opinion—or that of anyone else—why not find out for yourself? Do some homework and really examine what you have accepted as truth. Find out why you think the way you do.

Appendix B

Baptism in the Holy Spirit

I believe that the Bible teaches a baptism of the Holy Spirit. It comes after your baptism in the name of the Lord Jesus Christ. This is what is meant by being "Spirit-filled." In the book of Acts, we learn of Paul finding certain disciples who had not received the Holy Ghost—in fact, they had not even heard "whether there be any Holy Ghost." First, he baptized them in the name of Christ Jesus. Then he laid his hands on them and the Holy Ghost came on them and they spoke in tongues and prophesied. (Acts 19:1-6)

One weekend in November 2003, I enrolled in a mounted police class in which we were taught cavalry drills on horseback. While there I met a lovely Christian couple, Dana and Dirk. As we chatted, the Lord prompted me to ask if they had a desire to be baptized in the Holy Spirit. Dana exclaimed, "Here? In the parking lot?" Her husband agreed. Here is Dana's account of that experience:

The week of November 11, 2003 was the beginning of an explosive encounter with my Father God. I was firmly rooted in my beliefs, instilled through my traditional denomination. I was secure in my faith—knowing the first verse to several hymns and owning a study Bible with several words

115

I had underlined. In other words, what I had was religion, but what the Lord was about to teach me was relationship.

The week I met Caspar was a week filled with an intense, unusual desire to worship. I sensed God speaking to me in my spirit and felt he was preparing me for something. I kept hearing in my spirit the words, "You've been set loose." I attended a horse clinic that weekend and shared with Caspar what the Lord was doing. Caspar said he felt the Lord wanted me to receive the baptism of the Holy Spirit. His prayer was simple and short, and I began to experience intense tingling from my elbows to the tips of my fingers.

The days that followed were filled with an insatiable love for the Lord. There weren't enough hours in the day to worship him! My nights were filled with songs of praise, prophetic dreams and visions and beautiful anointed prayers. Over and over a word from the Lord was confirmed through friends. The Bible became alive to me, the words leaping off the pages in eye-opening revelation.

The Lord led me to pray and lay hands on a very sick woman who was in the hospital, scheduled for surgery. Within 24 hours, she received a complete healing from the Lord and her surgery was canceled.

For the first time in my life, I began to experience the love of my Father. Relationship took the place of religion. In Matthew 7:20, Jesus said, "Wherefore by their fruits ye shall know them." Since that day in November, my fruit is passion fruit! I seek to share my passion for God the Father, Jesus my Savior and the Holy Spirit with everyone and I pray this intense fire will never dim!

I share Dana's story with you in the hopes that if you have not been baptized with the Holy Spirit, you will earnestly seek that miracle in your own life. Sadly, many Christians have never asked for the Lord to anoint and baptize them as we are instructed to, and signs and wonders do not follow. No one gets healed. These dear brothers and sisters may still be going to heaven, but they lack understanding.

Did you know that Billy Graham has written a book on the subject? It is entitled, *The Holy Spirit*, and in it Dr. Graham says:

> "If you believe in Jesus Christ, a power is available to you that can change your life. Before the day of Pentecost, the emphasis was on the word "ask" (Luke 11:13). After Pentecost, the emphasis was on the word "receive" (Acts 2:38). This is the good news: we are no longer waiting for the Holy Spirit, He is waiting on us."[7]

Jesus himself gave us the foundation for the baptism in the Holy Spirit: that it is a separate experience from that of salvation and water baptism.

But ye shall receive power, after that the Holy Ghost is come upon you: and ye shall be witnesses unto Me both in Jerusalem, and in all Judea, and in Samaria and unto the uttermost part of the earth. (Acts 1:8)

Jesus has made it clear that in salvation, you are born again; you receive the Holy Spirit when you ask the Lord to come into your heart and save you. This is when we are "sealed with the Holy Spirit of promise." (Ephesians 1:13)

Baptism in the Holy Spirit is an entirely different experience from that of salvation. In Matthew 3:11, John the Baptist said about it, "I indeed baptize you with water unto repentance: but he that cometh after me is mightier than I, whose shoes I am not worthy to bear: he shall baptize you with the Holy Ghost, and with fire."

I don't know about you, but I have seen some believers act like they are afraid of accepting some gifts from the Lord. I cannot even relate to that concept anymore. I want every gift the Lord in His mercy and grace will give me. I accept every promise He made to you and me.

> *And when the day of Pentecost was fully come, they were all with one accord in one place. And suddenly there came a sound from heaven as of a rushing mighty wind, and it filled all the house where they were sitting. And there appeared unto them cloven tongues like as of fire, and it sat upon each of them. And they were all filled with the Holy Ghost, and began to speak with other tongues, as the Spirit gave them utterance. (Acts 2:1-4)*

Do you have a hard time believing that this baptism is necessary? Then read this excerpt from *Crisis Experience in the Lives of Noted Christians*, by V. R. Edam.

> "In the late 19th century, D. L. Moody attributed the success of his ministry to a dramatic spiritual experience he called his "baptism of the Holy Spirit." Moody wrote he had been crying out to God for the power of the Spirit. In response to his persistent prayer the Holy Spirit fell on him. "One day, in the city of New York — oh, what a day! I cannot describe it, I seldom refer to it; it is almost too sacred an experience to name. I can only say that God revealed Himself to me and I had such an experience of His love that I had to ask Him to stay His hand. I went to preaching again. The sermons were not different. I did not present any new truths and yet hundreds were converted. I would not now be placed back where I was before that blessed experience, if you should give me all the world."

Here is one final citing from Scripture on the difference between baptism with water and baptism with the Holy Spirit. Paul discovers some disciples on the road in Ephesus. And by implication, if they are disciples they are also believers. Look at what Paul said and did.

And it came to pass, that, while Apollos was at Corinth, Paul having passed through the upper coast came to Ephesus: and finding certain disciples, he said unto them, "Have ye received the Holy Ghost since ye believed?" And they said unto him, "We have not so much as heard whether there be any Holy Ghost." And he said unto them, "Unto what then were ye baptized?" And they said, "Unto John's baptism." Then said Paul, "John verily baptized with the baptism of repentance, saying unto the people, that they should believe on Him which should come after him, that is Christ Jesus." When they heard this, they were baptized in the name of the Lord Jesus. And when Paul had laid his hands upon them, the Holy Ghost came on them: and they spake with tongues, and prophesied. (Acts 19:1-6)

---

7. From *The Holy Spirit*, Billy Graham, published by Thomas Nelson Publishers

The Following report and EKG taken at Kennestone Hospital Emergency Room show my heart was diseased in 1998.

As far as I am aware there is no known cure for this disease. Unless the Lord in His, mercy, grace, and love heals you in the name of Jesus Christ of Nazareth.

Appendix C

Doctors' Reports

ECHOCARDIOGRAM REPORT

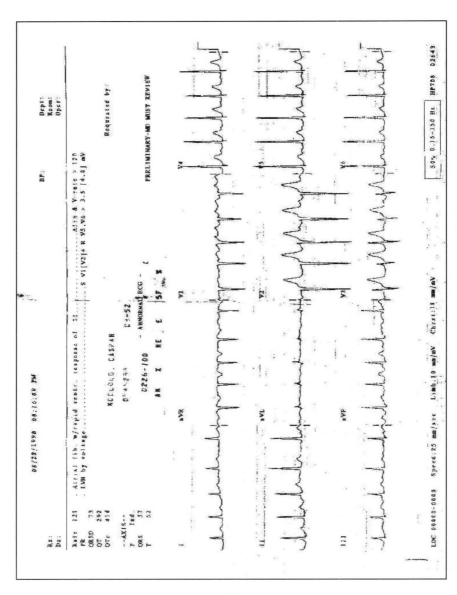

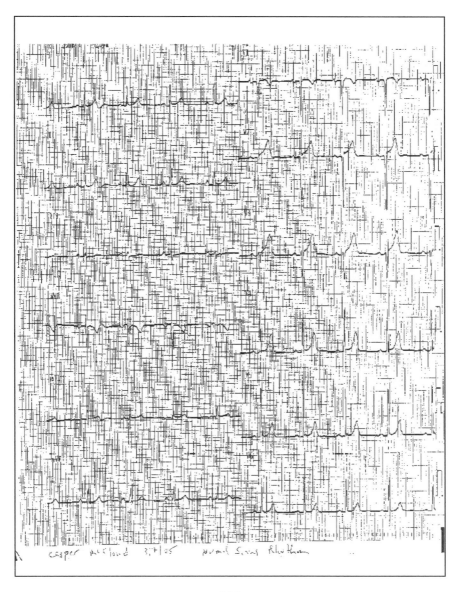

Appendix D

The following are eye—witness testimonies of recent events showing God's power, mercy, grace and love... This letter was written by my friend Randy Drone:

———————————————

Dear Friends,

It is important that I write this letter of witness regarding what I saw this past Sunday, June 26th 2005.

My dear friend Caspar McCloud phoned me about 9:30 a.m. to tell me that he was going to Montgomery, Alabama to visit his close friend and medical physician, Dr. Terri. Last Thursday Terri had been taking care of a neighbor's horse in her stable and had a terrible experience. The horse had somehow been spooked and had trampled Terri, sending her to the hospital. The blessing here is that she suffered no broken bones, but she appeared to be in a lot of pain from having her torso and limbs literally stomped on by this thousand pound horse.

Caspar asked me if I would go with him to pray for and lay hands on Terri that day. I gladly agreed to go with him. As we drove to Montgomery, Caspar told me of being asked a question by the Lord in his sleep the previous night. The question was, "Is it any harder for Me to heal after an accident than to heal from a disease?" Caspar responded, "No, all healing is the same for you, God; you can do anything." Caspar told me that this interaction with God convinced him that it was important to go to Terri in her time of need to pray for her and lay hands on her. As we arrived, we were greeted at the door by her husband George who gave us a first–hand account of what happened to her on Thursday and on the following days leading up to her present condition. She had been in bed since Thursday and had been in a lot of pain from internal injuries. There had been a concern about internal bleeding, but George thought that they were past that hurdle now. As we walked into Terri's room she was lying very quietly in a dark room with worship music playing softly in the background. It was a struggle for her to speak to us. Her voice was very soft and labored but she managed a smile and thanked us for driving to Montgomery to see her. Even smiling was difficult for her. Her pain was evident.

Caspar began to pray for Terri while George and I stood in agreement with him as he asked God for intervention in this situation and for divine healing for Terri's body. We stayed for a little while after we prayed to visit with Terri & George, to share our faith with each other, and to build understanding and relationship with each other and with God.

As we stayed and talked it became clear that Terri's voice was getting stronger and she wasn't struggling nearly as much to breathe. Her whole countenance was changing as we watched.

The next improvement came when she realized that she could move her left arm for the first time since the accident without any pain. She was smiling at this point from joy and the pain seemed to be much less. At this point Terri asked me about my experience at Pleasant Valley and wanted to know more about my healing from multiple sclerosis. She was very alert at this point and asked several questions from a medical perspective that demonstrated she was able to concentrate less on her pain and more on our conversation. Every time she demonstrated improvement, Caspar and I would just look at each other in amazement. We realized that we were witnessing the miracle we had just prayed for and we repeatedly thanked God for His mercy and love.

When Caspar finally decided that we should get on the road to return to Atlanta, Terri said she felt well enough to walk us to the car!! I was stunned. When we walked into her room earlier and saw her so debilitated and in such pain, I had no expectation that we would watch her walk out of that room before we left. I told her that she had nothing to prove and it might be best if she just stayed in bed to rest but she responded that she really felt like walking us out to the car. As she walked out of her room she commented that it was good to finally get a deep breath, especially one without pain. She stood there and walked around with no problems that I could see. We could see the joy of the Lord on her face when she smiled. It was awesome.

From Caspar

My friend Dr. Terri was badly hurt a few days ago, when a horse suddenly panicked and attacked her by rearing up and stomping on her multiple times. Try to imagine a 1000—pound animal knocking you down and then coming down on you repeatedly with great force. She is only 5'2" tall and is very petite. I praise God she was not killed. Fortunately her husband George was nearby at the time, and was able to pull her away before she was trampled to death. This is much to his credit as he was injured playing ball a few months ago and shattered his left elbow.

George telephoned me to tell me the news from the hospital. No bones had been broken but there was much concern about internal bleeding. Being a physician, she was allowed to go home hours later as her nursing staff took turns attending to her needs.

This morning I had an image of laying hands on her and the Lord healing her. I heard the Lord ask me a question, "Which is easier for Me to do? Heal someone of a so—called incurable disease like I did for you, or heal someone from an accident?" I knew straightway, and answered, "You are God Almighty and you can do anything. Nothing is impossible with you."

So I drove to Montgomery, Alabama with a brother name Randy Drone who was healed of MS at PVC in 2003. Randy is one of our staff members for our Sanctification Friday meetings. It took us 3½ hours to get there because it was raining hard and traffic was heavy. When we arrived, Dr. Terri looked very pale and was obviously in great pain. The room was dark and she was in bed looking like she would be there for at least the next month. There was praise music playing softly in the background. I heard my friend Phil Keaggy's song titled "The Love Broke Through." Randy was at the foot of the bed. I went to the side and simply held her hand and started praying. I felt enormous love and compassion from the Lord, and asked Him to pour out His extravagant love and heal her immediately in the name of Jesus Christ of Nazareth. She was breathing very shallowly and her voice was very raspy and weak when we arrived. She said her sides hurt with every breath she took since she had taken repeated blows to her rib cage and stomach area.

After the prayer, she found herself able to take a deep breath. Next, she discovered she could move her left arm without the pain, saying she had not been able to move her arm since the accident. I commented that her voice seemed to be returning and getting stronger. I then reminded her about a time when

129

I had prayed for her over the telephone several years ago and the Lord in His mercy, grace and love healed her instantly of pneumonia.

Randy started sharing his testimony and we kept encouraging her with the Word. All this time I had been holding her hand and when I let go, she took my hand again explaining she was gaining strength from holding my hand. So I kept at it. After about an hour, she was visibly transformed. Her eyes were now clear and the colour was back in her face. Soon she said she felt good enough to get out of bed. Within minutes she was walking around and giggling almost as if she had not been hurt at all. She was rather amazed at how good she now felt.

Randy and I kept looking at each other and praised God as we watched his awesome power unfold before us. Dr. Terri then walked us out to my car and wondered aloud if perhaps we should all go to the hospital and pray and watch the Lord empty out all the rooms there. She then sat down in a swing chair and waved to us as we headed back home.

Randy turned to me and said, "We just witnessed a miracle!" I said, "Yes we have, and wasn't it splendid the way the Lord did it all so naturally?" This is the Christian life. We commented that Pastor Henry would have asked us why we went to Alabama if we did not believe the Lord would heal her.

Randy told me later that was the first time he witnessed a miracle happening before his eyes. I knew in the natural it did not make sense to expect someone to be healed from an accident like that. But I tell you the Lord gave me the faith to believe for it. So I decided to just show up and do what I know to do and expect a miracle. Even though I did not know all the medical names like Pastor Henry, I figured the Lord would meet me where I was.

Pastor Henry has taught me great Bible truths, and I believe when we walk in obedience and faith now, supernatural events will take place. I also knew that I could count on my dear friend Pastor John Aldridge in Texas to cover us in prayer. (Jeremiah 33:3 — *Call unto Me, and I will answer thee, and show thee great and mighty things, which thou knowest not.*) I had asked a number of people to pray on my way there that morning and really felt the prayer coverage.

Mark 16 and Matthew 10:8 tell us that signs and wonders will follow the believer, and one of those wonders is laying hands on the sick and seeing them recover.

I tell you it is all true, as you well know.

In Christ's love,
Caspar

———————————————

Tuesday, July 19, 2005

Subject: Re: Thanks for sharing the love of Christ at the Harvest Centers

Linda,

Please let Caspar know that one man had had a migraine headache for 4 days. He was set free that night in Jesus' name. Another lady had back pain and it left when the peace of God filled her spirit.

Pastor Caspar McCloud blessed us with his testimony of being raised from the dead and his healing from an incurable disease. He shared how believers can come into agreement with evil spirits through lack of knowledge and become snared by the devil as described in 2 Timothy. The scripture reads:

2 Tim. 2:26 "And that they may recover themselves out of the snare of the devil, who are taken captive by him at his will."

Pastor Caspar led praise & worship to prepare the people's hearts to hear the Word of God and to receive their miracles. God is good.

Praises to Jesus from Harvest Centers:

"I had been suffering with a migraine headache for four days and nothing I was doing was making a difference. I listened to the message at last Friday night's gathering and afterward the speaker broke the pain in Jesus' name. He spoke the Word of God over me and I was set free from migraines for His glory."

"I came to the Friday night gathering for the first time last Friday night. I had pain radiating down through my back and the chiropractor had not been able to make it go away. A man laid hands on my back and neck. I felt peace enter my body and the pain in my back and neck left my body. Jesus is awesome."

Sanctification Fridays!

"The Spirit of the Lord is upon me, because he hath anointed me to preach the gospel to the poor: he hath sent me to heal the brokenhearted, to preach deliverance to the captives, and recovery of sight to the blind, to set at liberty them that are bruised, to preach the acceptable year of the Lord." — Jesus Christ of Nazareth

Luke 4:18, 19 KJV (from Isaiah 61:1, 2)

What does the Bible have to say about making us free from sin and disease?

Join us Fridays and find out!

We are a "mixed bag" of believers simply gathered together in the name of the Lord Jesus every Friday at 7:00 pm. The Church of the Messiah in Canton, GA, has kindly provided a location for us. We offer help, knowledge, insights and ministry for the healing and prevention of diseases of the spirit, soul and body.

Where is the Church of the Messiah?

415 Charles Cox Drive
Canton, GA 30115
telephone 770–475–5501

Directions from Atlanta via 575 North
Exit 16, Right onto GA 140 toward Roswell
Cross over East Cherokee Drive (Publix intersection)
Bear left onto Charles Cox Drive (sign for Church of the
Messiah)
Left onto Charles Cox Drive
Church is on the left.

Directions from Highway 400
Exit 7 onto Holcomb Bridge Road toward Roswell (becomes
East Crossville Road)
Right onto Crabapple Road
Left onto Arnold Mill Road/GA 140 eight miles
Right after the Habersham Bank, turn right onto very narrow
Charles Cox Road
Go 2/10th of a mile, cross over Batesville Road. Charles Cox
Road becomes Charles Cox Drive.
Church is on the left.

Contact Pastor Caspar and Joan McCloud at 770–475–
5501 for more information on the connection between
sanctification and health.

You can also visit www.pleasantvalleychurch.net

Sanctification Fridays! Join us for praise and worship,
teaching, sharing, fellowship and prayer.

Know anybody that needs to read Caspar's story?

To get more copies of this book,
go to www.CasparMcCloud.com

To order by mail, send check or money order to:

Praxis Press
3630 Thompson Bridge Road
Suite #15–100
Gainesville, GA 30506

Individual copies are $14.99 each.
Cases of 24 books are available for $12.75 per book ($306.00 per case).

For concert bookings
contact Linda by e–mail at:
livingnotes@comcast.net

For interview or talk show bookings
contact Clint by e–mail at:
info@praxispress.org

If you enjoyed this book, you may want to read other books from Praxis Press:

The Art of Listening Prayer
by Seth Barnes

If you're dying to hear God's voice, the good news is that you can! If God loves His people, couldn't it be that He desires to speak one–on–one with us? If so, wouldn't our first priority be to learn how to hear from Him?

It's one of the most important questions of our lives. Yet many of us settle for a one–way, humdrum monologue, in which we do all the talking and give God no time to speak back.

Explore what it means to experience prayer that really is two–way. Using the Bible as a foundation, you can go way beyond theory and grow in the practice of listening prayer. This interactive devotional is for the person who isn't satisfied with a dry faith.

About the Author

Seth Barnes is founder of Adventures in Missions, a ministry whose objective is to raise up a generation of radical disciples of Jesus Christ. He lives in Gainesville, Georgia.

Find out more at www.praxispublishing.com.